SO-DUT-325

Hamlet's Heirs

Namesake princes and presidents; stolen thrones and elections;
plutocrats and insurgents; campaign trails and war-mongering;
waning monarchy and imperilled democracy; and revengers,
early modern and postmodern – these themes drive this provocative study of Shakespeare's legacy in contemporary American
and British politics.

Linked by focused readings of *Hamlet* and the *Henriad*, the
essays follow Shakespeare's two most famous royal sons, the
princes Hamlet and Hal, as they haunt contemporary political
psychology in the early years of a new millennium, and especially
in the aftermath of September 11, 2001. Between devolution in
Britain and the new 'doctrine' of pre-emptive strike in the
United States, our contemporary Hamlets and Hals epitomize a
debate – as fraught now as in Shakespeare's day – about the cost
of spin-doctoring legacies. In exploring how current political
culture inherits Shakespeare, *Hamlet's Heirs* challenges scholarly
assumptions about historical periodicity, modernity, and the uses
of Shakespeare in present-day contexts.

Speaking to readers in a voice that is adventurous rather than
authoritative, innovative rather than institutional, and speculative rather than orthodox, Charnes reveals that when it comes to
legacy we are all, in one way or another, Hamlet's heirs.

ACCENTS ON SHAKESPEARE
General Editor: TERENCE HAWKES

It is more than twenty years since the New Accents series helped to establish 'theory' as a fundamental and continuing feature of the study of literature at the undergraduate level. Since then, the need for short, powerful 'cutting edge' accounts of and comments on new developments has increased sharply. In the case of Shakespeare, books with this sort of focus have not been readily available. **Accents on Shakespeare** aims to supply them.

Accents on Shakespeare volumes will either 'apply' theory, or broaden and adapt it in order to connect with concrete teaching concerns. In the process, they will also reflect and engage with the major developments in Shakespeare studies of the last ten years.

The series will lead as well as follow. In pursuit of this goal it will be a two-tiered series. In addition to affordable, 'adoptable' titles aimed at modular undergraduate courses, it will include a number of research-based books. Spirited and committed, these second-tier volumes advocate radical change rather than stolidly reinforcing the status quo.

IN THE SAME SERIES

Hamlet's Heirs

Shakespeare and the Politics of a New Millennium

LINDA CHARNES

Routledge
Taylor & Francis Group

NEW YORK AND LONDON

First published 2006 in the USA and Canada
by Routledge
270 Madison Ave, New York, NY 10016

Simultaneously published in the UK
by Routledge
2 Park Square, Milton Park, Abingdon, Oxon, OX14 4RN

Routledge is an imprint of the Taylor & Francis Group

© 2006 Linda Charnes

Typeset in Baskerville by
Integra Software Services Pvt. Ltd, Pondicherry, India
Printed and bound in Great Britain by
TJ International Ltd, Padstow, Cornwall

All rights reserved. No part of this book may be reprinted or
reproduced or utilised in any form or by any electronic, mechanical,
or other means, now known or hereafter invented, including
photocopying and recording, or in any information storage or retrieval
system, without permission in writing from the publishers.

British Library Cataloguing in Publication Data
A catalogue record for this book is available from the British Library

Library of Congress Cataloging in Publication Data
Charnes, Linda.
  Hamlet's heirs : Shakespeare & the politics of a new millennium /
Linda Charnes.
     p.   cm. — (Accents on Shakespeare)
  Includes bibliographical references and index.
  ISBN 0–415–26193–7 (alk. paper) — ISBN 0–415–26194–5 (pbk. : alk. paper)
  1. Shakespeare, William, 1564–1616. Hamlet.   2. Shakespeare, William,
  1564–1616—Political and social views.   3. Political plays, English—History and
  criticism.   4. Shakespeare, William, 1564–1616—Influence.   5. Politics and
  literature—Great Britain.   6. Inheritance and succession in literature.   7. Hamlet
  (Legendary character)   8. Monarchy in literature.   9. Princes in literature.
     I. Title.   II. Series.
PR2807.C2776 2006
822.3′3—dc22   2005030913

ISBN10: 0–415–26193–7   ISBN13: 978–0–415–26193–7 (hbk)
ISBN10: 0–415–26194–5   ISBN13: 978–0–415–26194–4 (pbk)

For Amanda and Jake

Contents

General editor's preface

In our time, the field of literary studies has rarely been a settled, tranquil place. Indeed, for over two decades, the clash of opposed theories, prejudices and points of view has made it more of a battlefield. Echoing across its most beleaguered terrain, the student's weary complaint 'Why can't I just pick up Shakespeare's plays and read them?' seems to demand a sympathetic response.

Nevertheless, we know that modern spectacles will always impose their own particular characteristics on the vision of those who unthinkingly don them. This must mean, at the very least, that an apparently simple confrontation with, or pious contemplation of, the text of a four-hundred-year-old play can scarcely supply the grounding for an adequate response to its complex demands. For this reason, a transfer of emphasis from 'text' towards 'context' has increasingly been the concern of critics and scholars since the Second World War: a tendency that has perhaps reached its climax in more recent movements such as 'New Historicism', 'Cultural Materialism' or 'Presentism'.

A consideration of the conditions – social, political or economic – within which the play came to exist, from which it derives and to which it speaks will certainly make legitimate demands on the attention of any well-prepared student nowadays. Of course, the serious pursuit of those interests will also inevitably start to undermine ancient and inherited prejudices, such as the supposed distinction between 'foreground' and 'background' in literary studies. And even the slightest awareness of the pressures of gender or of race, or the most cursory glance at the role played by that strange creature 'Shakespeare' in our cultural politics, will reinforce a similar turn towards questions that sometimes appear scandalously 'non-literary'. It seems clear that very different and unsettling notions of the ways in which literature might be addressed can hardly be avoided. The worrying truth is that nobody can just pick up Shakespeare's plays and read them. Perhaps – even more worrying – they never could.

The aim of *Accents on Shakespeare* is to encourage students and teachers to explore the implications of this situation by means of an engagement with the major developments in Shakespeare studies over recent years. It will offer a continuing and challenging reflection on those ideas through a series of multi- and single-author books which will also supply the basis for adapting or augmenting them in the light of changing concerns.

Accents on Shakespeare also intends to lead as well as follow. In pursuit of this goal, the series will operate on more than one level. In addition to titles aimed at modular undergraduate courses, it will include a number of books embodying polemical, strongly argued cases aimed at expanding the horizons of a specific aspect of the subject and at challenging the preconceptions on which it is based. These volumes will not be learned 'monographs' in any traditional sense. They will, it is hoped, offer a platform for the work of the liveliest younger scholars and teachers at their most outspoken and provocative. Committed and contentious, they will be reporting from the forefront of current critical activity and will have something new to say. The fact that each book in the series promises a Shakespeare inflected in terms of a specific urgency should ensure that, in the present as in the recent past, the accent will be on change.

Terence Hawkes

Acknowledgements

While writing this book, I benefited from presenting earlier versions of the material as talks and lectures. Among the most helpful forums were those provided by the Shakespeare Association of America (SAA) and The Folger Shakespeare Library. The SAA gave me frequent platforms for testing my ideas on panels and in seminars. In the spring of 1998 I directed a Folger seminar on 'Shakespeare and Postmodernism', which gave initial shape to the project, and I thank Barbara Mowat, Kathleen Lynch, and Lena Cowen Orlin for their support during that time.

Earlier versions of several chapters appeared, respectively, in *Shakespeare Quarterly* 48:1, 1997; *Philosophical Shakespeares*, ed. John Joughin (Routledge, 2000); and *Shakespeare and Modernity: Early Modern to the Millennium*, ed. Hugh Grady (Routledge, 2000). These three essays (the foundations of Chapters 3, 4, and 5) have been considerably revised, and brought up to date, for inclusion here.

Many friends and colleagues responded to this work with useful criticism, enthusiasm, and encouragement. Several chapters benefited, at earlier stages, from readings by Barbara Mowat, Hugh Grady, John Joughin, and Peter Stallybrass. I am most grateful to Susan Gubar, who read and commented on nearly the entire manuscript, and whose advice, criticism, and friendship have been invaluable. Liz Thompson at Routledge never doubted that this project would come to fruition, and I appreciate her tact and kindness. Indiana University, Morton Lowengrub, Kenneth Johnston, Stephen Watt, and IU's College Arts and Humanities

Institute were instrumental in providing support for grants and leave time to work on this book.

When writing about controversial matters – about literature, politics, the profession, or the process of writing itself – the support of friends and colleagues helps reinforce the courage of one's convictions. For conversations and exchanges that reinforced mine, I thank especially Susan Gubar and Barbara Hodgdon, as well as Catherine Belsey, Tom Cartelli, Margreta de Grazia, Christy Desmet, Polly Dodson, Mary Favret, Don Gray, Jeff Isaac, Jon Kamholz, Dennis Kennedy, Barbara Klinger, Richard Levin, Bryan Loughrey, Jaya Nilamani, Sharon O'Dair, Robert Sawyer, Janet Sorensen, Peter Stallybrass and Wayne Storey. I am deeply grateful to Adam Phillips for conversations about writing and for the inspiration of his work. For loving moral support, I thank James Charnes, Emily Charnes, Helga Hayse, Julia Michael, and Julie Weaver. Lastly, Terence Hawkes edited the manuscript line by line, and offered sharp and insightful criticism throughout. He gives new meaning to the notion of 'Patience on a Monument'.

1
Introduction: *Passing which Torch?*

> As a rule, people stick to their positions for anything but
> 'rational' reasons. What can be done?
>   – Peter Sloterdijk, *Critique of Cynical Reason*

The essays in this book were begun during what I thought was a
pivotal moment in American culture: the last decade of the
millennium, ushered in at the beginning by the Los Angeles race
riots and the Clarence Thomas–Anita Hill hearings and ushered
out by the Clinton Impeachment and 'Indecision 2000' – the
Supreme Court 'election' of George W. Bush. There were a
great many questions about the last decade of the century that
still needed addressing; but then came the terrorist attacks of
September 11, 2001, and suddenly many of these inquiries
became 'off-limits'. People spoke of 9-11 as if it represented an
'epistemological break' from the cultural traumas that had immediately preceded it: as if Osama Bin Laden, and not the Supreme
Court, had made George W. Bush a 'legitimate' President and
the entire sordid business of the election was now officially
'behind us', as if the terrorist attacks so entirely changed the
fabric of the nation that anything we did could be contained
within the elastic carapace of 'Operation Enduring Freedom',
including a unilateral invasion two years later of a country that
had nothing to do with those attacks.

I wondered whether the several essays of this book begun
prior to 9-11 would be consonant with anything I could write after
the attacks and during 'Operation Iraqi Freedom'. For months

I waited, paralyzed with rage and shame – in other words, *Hamlet-like* – at what I considered to be our illegitimate leader's actions, to see what the outcome of our unilateral Iraqi invasion would be, or whether we would finally capture the real culprit, Osama bin Laden. I waited to see if developments would render irrelevant my arguments about the increasingly *constitutive* irrationality of American culture. After all, many people, smarter and more prominent than I, were repeating like a mantra that 'everything had changed'; and so I watched and waited for the promised 'paradigm shift' (or image of that horror).

What I have since come to believe, however, is that far from triggering an epistemological break in American culture, 9-11 and its subsequent fallout have revealed a deep structural connection between the notorious events that rang out the millennium and those that blasted us into the twenty-first century – that the spectacle of social and political trauma that characterized the 1990s was in fact 'a moment of origin' for what has since unfolded.[1] The events of September 11 did not 'change' things so much as they abruptly shoved an already rough beast out of what remained of its hiding.

This structural continuity can best be characterized by what philosopher Peter Sloterdijk, in his history of post-Enlightenment ideology critique, calls 'cynical idealism', or 'Enlightened False Consciousness'.[2] Cynical idealism, Sloterdijk explains, is a condition in which people harbour 'a permanent doubt about their own activities' yet mask their doubt with the brittle bravado of idealist enthusiasm (1987: 5). They know that their motivations and reasoning will no longer hold up to scrutiny, but their reservations are cast aside by an even more insistent re-subscription to their original dubious positions. In fact, the more untenable the position is *clearly shown to be* (for example, 'Intelligent Design' versus evolution, or the presence of weapons of mass destruction in Iraq), the more vehemently it is maintained – not because people do not 'know better' (although arguably some do not) but precisely because they do know better and it doesn't matter. As Slavoj Žižek puts it:

> They know very well what they are doing, but still, they are doing it. Cynical reason is no longer naive, but is a paradox of enlightened false consciousness: one knows the falsehood very

well, one is well aware of a particular interest behind an ideological universality, but still one does not renounce it.[3]

In an age of vast media infiltration, few can claim ignorance about the questionable, unethical, and frequently illegal operations of big corporations and government. Claiming to be 'in the dark' is, for anyone who reads a newspaper or owns a television or surfs the Internet, no longer a believable option.

Consequently, unlike the old Marxian notion of 'false consciousness', in which underlings are duped into thinking that those they labour under have their best interests at heart, 'enlightened false consciousness' involves *knowingly* choosing to adhere to an ideological fantasy out of a resigned conviction of its inevitable triumph ('it would happen anyway, even if I went against the mainstream'). In this scenario, people tacitly consent out of convenience and attempt to put 'a good face on things', or to convince themselves that the motives of those 'at the top' do not really matter since, in the last instance, 'everyone' benefits from the system anyway (even if, as Hurricane Katrina has so graphically revealed, they do not).[4]

What perhaps began as political *naivete*, or an inability to 'connect the dots', has become a refusal, structurally underwritten by the way the mass media presents information. As Sloterdijk puts it,

> We live in a world that brings things into false equations, produces false samenesses of form and false samenesses of values (pseudoequivalences) between everything and everyone, and thereby also achieves an intellectual disintegration and indifference in which people lose the ability to distinguish correct from false, important from unimportant, productive from destructive, because they are used to taking the one for the other (1987: 314).

Pseudoequivalences are everywhere: while CNN announces the London bombings of July 7, 2005, the 'crawl' at the base of the screen ceaselessly announces such simultaneous 'news' as the box office profits for 'War of the Worlds', and the actor Brad Pitt's bout with flu. In a culture in which all kinds of information are presented simultaneously as if they were equally noteworthy, the critical ability to differentiate between what is worth paying attention to and what is not is gradually eroded, and the ability to assess the credibility of certain claims is hobbled. We can see this merely as faulty reasoning or as a deliberate strategy on the part of those who have the most to gain by such pseudoequivalences:

> In the last instance, cynicism leads back to the amoral equating of different things. Those who do not see the cynicism evident when press reports on torture in South America are placed between perfume ads will also not perceive it in the theory of surplus-value, even if they have read it a hundred times (Sloterdijk 1987: 315).

Currently of course we read about Abu Ghraib, or Guantanamo, or the New Orleans Superdome, between those perfume ads. This is not the same as false consciousness; in the grip of cynical idealism, people always already know better, yet permit actions to be undertaken in the *name* of an idealist position. For example, a unilateral invasion driven by a son's desire for revenge and his debt to oil interests is translated into a basic duty to liberate oppressed Iraqis and bring them the joys of democracy ('Operation Iraqi Freedom'). Or, a failure to locate the mastermind of terrorist attacks ultimately does not matter because we have 'brought the terrorist front to the enemy' ('The Global War on Terror', or, if one prefers, 'The Struggle Against Global Extremism'). Such 'swaps' are paralogisms, rhetorical sleights of hand that skilfully deploy sentimentalist structures of feeling to cement the switch.

Cynicism has another strategy, even more sinister: the ability to appropriate critique for its own purposes. Cynicism, as Sloterdijk says, is 'cheekiness that has changed sides', anticipating its opponents' criticisms and undercutting them by beating them to the punch. Recently, George W. Bush's office produced a 'comedy sketch' for the 2004 Press Club dinner, in which Bush crawled around on his hands and knees in the Oval Office, looking under his desk: 'those Weapons of Mass Destruction have to be here somewhere'. Ten years ago this would have been a *Saturday Night Live* parody with a Bush impersonator; but here we have Bush gamely poking fun at 'himself'. This might have been very amusing if thousands of people had not died and were not continuing to die as a result of the US and British invasion of Iraq (most of them the very civilians we claim to want to 'liberate').

The *stunning cynicism* of this spectacle failed to provoke popular outrage; on the contrary, it was enthusiastically received with knowing smiles and laughter by the press and guests at the dinner, and virtually shrugged off by news agencies (which briefly ran the tape for the general public to see. No outcry ensued).

Thus cynical idealism in the form of self-irony becomes a pseudoequivalent of actually changing course on foreign policy. Timothy Bewes, who has written on the history of cynicism, is correct when he says that historically, 'from its earliest appearance in Athens in the fifth century BC, cynicism has signified a spirit of antagonism towards cultural values' (1997: 1). The strange spin that cynical idealism puts on contemporary cynicism, however, is that what should be antagonism towards dominant cultural values becomes instead a vehement insistence on those values in spite of vivid evidence of the damage wrought in their name. No longer about 'disillusionment', cynical idealism reverses the standard order of cynicism, which begins with investment in ideals and ends in disillusionment and withdrawal. Cynical idealists begin from a position of *constitutive* disillusionment, knowing (or suspecting) that 'values-discourse' is only politically useful so long as one does not look too closely at what would be required to put it into practice.

It perhaps sounds disingenuous to say I had hoped I would be wrong. I had hoped that the more the crimes of those 'at the top' were revealed, the more outraged American citizens would become and the less willing they would be to permit business to proceed as usual. From rampant corporate scandals to an entirely unjustified war, I thought that the structure of political corruption underwriting these events would, when laid bare for all to see, be rejected. But in November 2004, with no weapons of mass destruction found in Iraq, with American soldiers dying daily in a rising insurgency (not to mention Iraqi civilian casualties), with an economic deficit of enormous proportions raising a catastrophic spectre for generations to come, and with no link between Al Quaeda and Iraq uncovered, George W. Bush was re-elected to the presidency, this time with the majority of the popular vote.

Admittedly this 'majority' was slim, since roughly 65 per cent of the electorate does not bother to vote at all. Nonetheless, even those Americans who are against the administration's policies and practices, as well as the true 'silent majority' who refuse to show up at the polls, have permitted the situation to continue. It is of course a generalization to talk about 'Americans' as if they were one unified body when in fact the nation is multifaceted, splintered, and divided about many issues; and some people will no doubt object to being 'lumped in' to my formulations about those who have supported the current regime.[5] Certainly, to some extent I am generalizing; but in terms of how the United States operates in the world, in terms of how it carries out foreign policies and is perceived by other nations, 'America' is viewed as one gigantic behemoth, irrespective of individual citizens' votes or political views. All Americans are implicated in the global legacies their nation's policies generate; no one can gainsay the fact that we will all inherit the legacy of what 'America' does at home and abroad. Even those who voted for the other guy will, like Prince Hal, have to 'pay the debt we never promised'.

Some readers might ask why Shakespeare needs to be central to a book concerned with contemporary political culture, why the plays are being 'used' in such a context. Apart from the fact that all Shakespeare scholars 'use' Shakespeare no matter what their approach (and my sense that it is fine to 'use' him), I will add that Shakespeare's plays provide the best models I know for mapping the political psychology of monarchy or oligarchy as it grinds against the increasingly insistent forms of discontent that eventually led, in 1776, to American secession from the British Empire. The friction between inherited and corporate forms of entitlement and the basic needs of citizens/subjects persists, nearly unabated, to this day, although in more easily misrecognized forms. The sharp poignancy of reading *Hamlet* and the *Henriad* in the present situation lies in the ways in which we have *failed* to realize and protect the truly radical democratic potential hinted at in these plays. Consequently, the 'wormholes' between the 'early modern' era and our own are worth exploring – inseparably a part of creating what William Bouwsma has called 'a usable past' (1990).

At the turn of the millennium, something in American (and, arguably, British) politics and culture began to 'mutate', and this mutation will have a profound impact on how we will read all kinds of texts in years to come. If Shakespeare's plays are going to matter to the future as anything more than a 'salute' to the past, they will have to matter differently. I will, presumably, be granted the right to wear my cap as a Shakespeare scholar. With regard to my arguments on American and British politics, I can only say, in the words of comedian Dennis Miller, 'that's just my opinion – and I could be wrong'.[6]

> *Every dead man is probably still alive somewhere.*
> – Fernando Pessoa[7]

The essays in this book grapple with inheritance, death, sex, procreation, debt, obligation, resurrections, insurrections, campaign trails, war-mongering, and legacies. Thematically linked by the anxieties triggered by England's laws of 'perpetual entail' – the system of primogeniture, patrilineal succession, and direct inheritance between the generations that structured and vexed Shakespearean culture – the essays explore Shakespeare's influence on contemporary beliefs about 'legacy'.

We have never, arguably, been less certain about what one generation owes another. In contemporary America, what exactly is the role of primogeniture? To what extent does it still organize our fantasies of leadership, even as an allegorical form? In Britain, where devolution, Blairism, and different nationalisms chafe against each other, the legacy of royalty has never been on shakier ground. Must children pay their fathers' (and mothers') symbolic debts? How are compromised legacies to be managed and deployed? How, and to what extent, does the process of handing something 'down' change its basic nature, and conversely, how does the substance of a legacy change the hearts, minds, and social relationships of those who take it on? Do legacies have intrinsic statutes of limitation, and if not, should they? How do we arrest their momentum if their size and weight become crushing? What is involved in creating a legacy in the first place and, more importantly, why does it seem to matter so much?

Perhaps it would be useful here to differentiate between legacy and inheritance, terms that are sometimes used interchangeably. Although the Latin *legare* does suggest a bequeathal, the term is most broadly understood as a function of office. A legate is technically a deputy, entrusted to carry a message or an embassy on behalf of someone else. In an etymological sense, one cannot choose or craft one's own legacy (despite what many current and ex-presidents would like to believe). Legacies, to the extent that they convey *messages*, are largely out of one's hands and are dependent upon the passage of time to assign their particular form. A legacy is always bequeathed retroactively. Whereas the theatre of inheritance is familial (even when, as in monarchies, it is also political), legacy's theatre is historical and social. By 'inheritance', I mean the material transmission of property, monies, lands, biological characteristics, and the intergenerational management and disposition of goods. By 'legacy', I mean something much trickier: the largely symbolic (although also frequently material) demands *of* the past, enunciated *by* the future, *to* the present. A legacy is not what has been but what *will have been* as the present imagines its relationship to the past through the 'eyes' of the future. Legacies are the past's way of keeping unfulfilled desires alive, whether they are reasonable, unreasonable, or monstrous.

The essays here concentrate on the legacies bequeathed to Shakespeare's two most famous, and culturally durable, royal sons: the princes Hal and Hamlet. Both have highly vexed relations to monarchy in particular and to paternalism in general; but each has beqeathed to us a drastically different model of the social and psychological politics of succession. Prince Hal is a namesake who must successfully inherit a throne gained illegitimately by his father. Prince Hamlet is the namesake of a legitimate king who, despite being dead, refuses to 'give up the ghost' of his power. Taken together, the two princes epitomize the debate – as fraught in our own day as in Shakespeare's – about the duties, dangers, and burdens of inheriting, and spin-doctoring, legacies. How, for example, does the crisis of legitimacy in the second tetralogy prefigure contemporary American electoral politics? How does a slacker-prince's unwillingness to take his father's place inform contemporary Britain's attitudes towards its waning monarchy? What is the role of the filial Revenger in the American cultural imagination? Why is it that the United States, a supposedly populist democracy, continues compulsively to enact fantasies of monarchy while Britain, one of the world's oldest monarchies, struggles with fantasies of democratic populism? These essays demonstrate the degree to which the princes Hal and Hamlet continue to haunt the stage of a millennial culture still organized by patriarchal primogeniture (both filial and symbolic).

Hamlet, however, has special pride of place in this book – the prince whose individual bloodline has no future, and who has no one to whom he can 'will' anything. The termination of his family line is inseparable from the death of Denmark, as Fortinbras's presence and army make clear. With neither offspring nor political structures to entail, Hamlet faces an erasure of existence in both the literal and the symbolic realms, a threat of obliteration more complete than anything he could have imagined in his 'suicide' speech. To die and go we know not where is not as bad as *to die and go nowhere*. Consequently, it is not surprising that he asks Horatio to tell his 'story to the yet unknowing world'. A wounded name is better than no name at all. Perhaps this is what revenge is most deeply about: transforming the status of a name from victim to victor, erasing the emasculating effects of victimhood and replacing them with the more virile qualities of agency and influence. It is a rare revenger who does not want to have the last word. For Horatio, the task will be to generate a 'usable past' out of an unusable one: to turn a mess into a message and a thwarted inheritance into a respectable legacy.

Hamlet and Hal each embody 'all the contradictions', as Richard Wilson has put it, 'within Renaissance subjectivity between paternal freedom and filial obedience, a father's right to create identity and a child's duty to acquiesce in one imposed', tensions that 'collide in the threats of disinheritance which are spring-boards for so many Shakespearean plots' (Wilson 1993: 212). If (as Chapter 3 will argue) there are always two fathers – one who represents disembodied authority, justice, impartiality, and absolute integrity, and another who wallows in the pleasure of his arbitrary and corrupt power, then there are also always two sons – one who steps up to pay the father's debt and another who prefers not to. In Hamlet and Hal we have, respectively, a legitimate prince who inherits nothing from his father but his name and the command to 'Remember me', and a belated and involuntary prince who transforms his inheritance of the crown into a legacy: the ideological fantasy that will become 'England'.

A namesake prince seeks revenge on behalf of his father; but before he manages to kill the real culprit he destroys just about everyone else around him and in the process destroys his nation. He is then trumpeted as a hero. If this shoe still fits, then we are all Hamlet's heirs. Each of us privileged enough to participate in a democratic culture must wrestle with the ghosts of undead monarchs who seem endlessly to demand something of us. Puzzled legatees, we simultaneously bear a sense of frustrated entitlement to what we feel our culture 'owes' us, while we remain largely unwilling to claim responsibility for the things done in our collective name. Inheritors of cultural legacy all, we are entangled in 'perpetual entail' whether we like it or not. As Hamlet understood, it will matter to the future how we tell 'our story'.

The organizing strategy of this book is essayistic by design. While each essay stands on its own as an independent meditation on Shakespeare and cultural politics, they are bound together through applied readings of *Hamlet* and the *Henriad*, and by their shared orbit around the central themes of legacy, inheritance, succession, patrimony, and gender. Given the volatility of these matters in the present, I prefer the essay's more speculative and adventurous form to the limitations of an overarching linear argument. Although the essays focus on Shakespearean texts and figures, my concerns throughout are with their contemporary implications. To write from this standpoint is not to be 'unhistoricist' but to wear one's historicism with a difference. Reading Shakespeare for the present is no less valuable than 'historicizing' Shakespeare in his own context. There is room in Shakespeare studies for the contributions of various approaches. Since Chapter 2, 'The Fetish of "the Modern"', takes up the current debate between 'paid-up Presentists' and historicists and lays out my views on method, periodicity, and institutional 'Big Others', I will make only some prefatory remarks here.[8]

Writing less as a 'presentist' (a term I dislike) than as a paid-up Montaignean with an admitted bent towards theoretical unorthodoxy, I think that if one has a decent sense of critical smell it is not always a bad idea to follow one's nose. I expect, and even hope, to disagree with some of my own arguments in the not-so-distant future. Nonetheless, I have attempted to discern aspects of Shakespeare's culture that continue to be played out, with surprising force, in our own. Some may see this as a 'tranhistorical' or worse, an 'essentialist' goal; but we must recognize that there are certain historical repetition-compulsions that nations, as well as individuals, seem to enact. Tom Nairn puts it hauntingly well in his discussion of the persistence of nationalism:

> We know now how little genetics has to do with it, but the societal equivalent of DNA is another matter. There is a long-range transmission of community from one age into another, through a myriad of idioms and altering channels, which is too little understood. This can be seen as a cultural blood-stream too, sometimes blind or disguised in its impact, liable to assume unforeseeable shapes or even flow in reverse, and capable of rising to the surface when least expected.[9]

Nairn's formulation gives a 'real' historian's (rather than a 'new historicist's') blessing to a way of reading history as much for its enduring patterns – which he evocatively calls 'a cultural blood-stream' – as for its chronological moment. The 'long-range transmission of community', which flows in both directions depending on which 'channel' one tracks, certainly is 'too little understood'; but Nairn's words reinforce my sense that paradigms often disappear, only to re-emerge, sometimes several 'eras' later, in 'unforeseeable shapes'.

How then will we recognize them? We can start by acknowledging up front that human beings will always be ambivalent about the people they profess to love the most, and will always be disturbed by the blessings and curses of obligation, gifts, entailment, inheritances, and legacies. The most powerful figures in public life will usually, if not always, be hiding another 'version' of themselves, one more nasty, brutish, weak, and genuine than the personae they project in their public performances. Self-interest will always drive most (but certainly not all) behaviour. These aspects of human life tend not to change much over time. Their local configurations, however, are always changing; and different moments in history put surprising spins on familiar behaviour and structures of feeling. Sometimes a different spin is enough to generate fresh insight.

One takes risks investing in analysis for the present. An historicist can, with the confidence of hindsight, more easily produce 'authoritative' arguments based on causes and effects, events and results, than can someone who writes while the outcome of events is still uncertain. I think it is a risk worth taking, whether our range of reference is two, ten, or twenty years; for by risking we confront directly the shaping concerns of our own lifetime. On the one hand, we live in a democracy, presumably no longer politically organized by patrimonial succession. On the other (to paraphrase Pessoa), every Hamlet is probably still alive somewhere.

2
The Fetish of 'the Modern'

Over the last twenty-five years, literary scholars (in our efforts to get some respect from university administrators as well as average taxpayers) have felt under increasing pressure to justify what we do as properly contributing to society's 'knowledge base'. Pierre Bourdieu, in his analysis of the French university system, describes the 'forms of co-optation' that 'ensure the durable homogeneity of the habitus' of the academic disciplines. Bourdieu tells us that in universities as they are currently constituted,

> on the one hand, we have knowledge in the service of order and power, aiming at the rationalization, in both senses, of the given order; on the other hand we have knowledge confronting order and power, aiming not at putting public affairs in order but at analyzing them as they are ....[1]

Between these two hands, Bourdieu reserves a special place for the 'arts faculty', who he claims have 'a privileged vantage-point' for observing the struggle between the two kinds of university power, the social 'sciences' and the 'hard' sciences, both of which 'tend to impose themselves more or less uncontested' (73). For Bourdieu, literary studies, for example, challenges the binaristic division of 'competencies'.

However, I do not think our position is as privileged as Bourdieu would like to think: those of us who work in the 'humanities' have always had a hard time convincing those whose knowledge can be supported by statistics and 'data' that there is a method to our madness, or even a method to our method.

Tired of being the social sciences' 'poor relations', literary studies has increasingly situated itself within the same 'division of the knowledge faculties' Bourdieu describes. In doing so, we have adopted within our own borders a similar disrespect for work that does not conform to the standard 'division of competencies'. This has been especially true, I think, of many 'historicists' and 'materialists'; but before I clarify my own relationship to these developments, I will offer some speculations as to why many literary critics have become so invested in the doctrine of rigorous verification.

For the last few years, there has been an upswing in mutual dismissal – what I have come to think of as the Methodological SmackDown.[2] The (now old) 'new historicism' has come under fire for its formulaic predictability. Scholars motivated by an openly contemporary agenda (inelegantly labeled 'presentists') are criticized for not being formulaic enough – for not 'historicizing'. On yet another front, those interested mainly in theoretical or philosophical issues have been accused of perpetuating a new formalism in disguise. It seems to me that driving the SmackDown between historicism, presentism, psychoanalysis, and theory in general is an ideological fantasy of some kind of critical holy grail: in Lacanese, a methodological Big Other (the Critic-Supposed-to-Know) that will render our arguments authoritative and impregnable, both to challenge and to the inevitable irrelevance wrought by the passage of time. While historicists concern themselves with 'proving arguments' and 'mounting cases' based on verifiable evidence, 'presentists' want to use the past as a departure point for jumping into the cultural game while it is still being played out. The authority of the past 'as it really was' versus its pliable deployability in the present moment: thick description/reconstruction versus timely/polemical intervention.

Admittedly, I am simplifying the debate here, since many scholars operate between these divisions; and of course feminist and race scholars often use a range of critical and theoretical materials both to reconstruct the past and to critique the present. However, most literary scholars still feel compelled to apply a methodological label to what they are doing; and in my view, the SmackDown is less about the 'content' of any particular method than it is about the institutional (and political) psychology of labeling – how we organize ourselves as communities, as well as commodities, in the scholarly marketplace.

Since I lack the ability to settle the current debate about methods, I would rather situate it within what I see as a larger labeling problem: that of 'periodicity'. What virtually all scholars working in literary studies tend to share, whether historicists or presentists, is a tacit acceptance that there is such a 'thing' as 'Modernity': each camp tends to assume that the category of 'the modern' – with its attendant remoras of pre, early, high, and post – continues to be an accurate and useful way of determining how we read complex cultural texts. For example, the 'early modern' period in western culture is organized to include various 'sub-eras' called, respectively, the Renaissance, the Reformation, the Restoration, the Enlightenment, the Age of Reason, the Age of Revolution. Each of these labels indexes a set of intellectual, religious, artistic, economic, political and scientific criteria. For historians, the term 'early modern' has long been used to designate a series of practices. Phenomena such as guild memberships, plague effects, city formations, enclosure acts, demographic migration, child-rearing, econonomic transactions, and changing modes of production are examples of material from which historians construct their narratives.

As literary scholars adopted the historian's nomenclature, thematically flexible ways of organizing time became unfashionable. Neatly folded into the portmanteau label of 'modernity', these developments and sub-eras could conveniently be rendered chronologically syntagmatic and 'progressive', as if each sub-era somehow depended upon and reinforced the other in lockstep. Although the term 'Renaissance' is now regarded as unfashionably elitist, the term 'early modern' carries its own biases worthy of examination. Douglas Bruster points to the unease that attends our use of 'the early modern' as a category: 'Seemingly a simple phrase, "early modern" betrays some of its complexity even in the understated tension between its components: "early," which takes time in one direction, and "modern", which leads it in another.'[3] The very notion of 'the modern' is field-specific and field-invented, and includes widely, if not wildly, divergent time frames depending on where one is located in the 'knowledge faculties'. To a physical anthropologist, for example, the modern period begins roughly 6.5 million years ago. To a Chinese historian, the 'early Modern period' begins with the Opium War of 1840, and the 'Modern' period runs from the May 4th Cultural Movement of 1919 up to the present day.[4] For different disciplines, and in non-western cultures, 'the modern' is not tethered to the emergence of capitalism, or the New Science, or the Industrial Revolution.

In fact, the word 'modern' did not originally have any particular content at all. As Margreta de Grazia puts it, 'The word's function was once exclusively deictic: its signification, like that of today, now, at present, depended on the time of its utterance.'[5] According to de Grazia, the latinate and vernacular usage of 'modern' denoted 'timeliness', things that are of 'the present moment'. To be timely is to have current value or relevance. The transformation of 'modern' from an adjective capable of a rolling embrace of the present moment into an epistemological category that places epochs in temporal containers is a function solely of the discourse of western Enlightenment. The western concept of 'modernity' implies something that has been updated and improved, even detached, from what has come before. With its implicit foundation in the New Science and its explicit reference to 'progress', the term 'early modern', as Richard Halpern points out, 'has become increasingly associated with a kind of positivist historicism which rejects all contexts or meanings other than the original ones as "ahistorical" or "anachronistic"'.[6]

Worse, our current notion of modernity privileges, and naturalizes, a strictly Eurocentric and western vision of historical development. Without the fetish of 'the modern', categories such as 'first world', third world', and 'developing' nations would make no sense. Even as literary scholars have critiqued and unmasked the naked will to power behind the doctrine of Manifest Destiny, our use of the current concept of 'modernity' reproduces it by continuing to underwrite a progressivist philosophy in which 'underdeveloped' nations must be led to 'catch up' with us, even if we have to invade and bomb them into it.[7] Although what scholars mean by the 'modern period' is not identical to what the average person-on-the-street means by 'modern', there is enough overlap between academic and colloquial usages to reinforce the conflation of our late capitalist standard of living with idealist (and increasingly doctrinal) terms such as 'freedom', 'liberty', and 'democracy'.[8]

'Modernity' has morphed into a category that denotes the practices largely of twentieth-century western culture. The establishment and perpetuation of this definition has given it a veneer of authoritative reality; and historians, with their reference to the bedrock of 'facts', have been granted special status within the humanities as a result. The new historicist movement in literary studies was at least as much an effort to capitalize on the institutional prestige of historians as it was an abreaction against the 'New Criticism'. The competitive politics of institutional Oedipalism requires the invention of new 'isms'. If the sciences – with their endless vista of new discoveries – provide the benchmark for what intellectual 'progress' should look like, then the humanities, including literary criticism, must keep up appearances. If we cannot just 'invent' ideas (the charge levelled at the Formalists and the New Critics), we can turn to the more valued status of historical facts. Historians' mimetic relationship to the procedural gestures of the sciences has granted them a privileged status in relation to 'knowledge' that literary scholars, no matter how inventive, have had difficulty matching. In the stampede to avoid the stigma of Formalism, many Renaissance scholars adopted what they saw as the methods, values, and nomenclatures of historians (an incursion that did not go unnoticed, or unresented, by 'real' historians in history departments).

Thus we adopted the historians' ready-made term for our period: it was 'early modern'. When exactly the 'early modern period' begins and ends, or segues into the foyer of the 'modern period', has eluded even the most punctilious of historicists. Therefore, while we cannot actually point to anything concrete, we still know (vaguely) what we mean by the phrase 'early modern', because we can corral our 'criteria' into three arenas: the emergence of mercantile capitalism and a money economy; the emergence of the ideology of the atomized individual, to which the Protestant reformation, print culture, and expanding literacies gave rise; and the development of the New Science, with its medical, physical, and industrial revolutions. Hence the criteria of content are installed in a word originally meant to be infinitely adaptable to the present, emptying it not only of portable flexibility but also of contestability. This last might have been precisely the point.

Meanwhile, as we focus our attention on early capitalism, enclosure acts, the politics of print culture, literacy, and the values of the industrial revolution so that we may better 'critique' the operations of power 'back then', the real power brokers of our administration manipulate *exactly the same things* in the present in order to maintain their stranglehold on resources and privilege. My point here is *not* to say that literary scholars are 'in league with' those brokers but to illustrate the fact that we accept the same frames of reference, however differently we may deploy them. As Bruno Latour succinctly puts it, 'questions of episte-mology are also questions of social order'.[9] We have not paid adequate attention to this; and any critique of 'periodicity' must take questions of epistemology seriously.

In *We Have Never Been Modern*, Latour describes the establishment of 'the Modern Constitution' as it emerged in mid-seventeenth-century Britain. By 'Modern Constitution', Latour means the laws, assumptions (spoken and unspoken), and strategies used by the self-styled 'moderns' to categorize and control legitimate and illegitimate forms of knowledge. As his founding fathers of modernity, Latour chooses Robert Boyle and Thomas Hobbes. Boyle, inventor of the vacuum-pump, is credited with the invention of the modern laboratory, in which phenomena could be 'produced artificially in [a] closed and protected space' and tested and analysed under completely controlled conditions (Latour 1993: 18). In case the 'facts' produced in the theatre of his laboratory are insufficiently persuasive, Boyle has backup: he invites 'credible, trustworthy, well-to-do witnesses to the scene of the experiments to attest to their veracity' (ibid.).

Then there is Hobbes, who 'rejected Boyle's entire theatre of proof' and who mostly wanted to see an end to the civil wars fracturing seventeenth-century English society (ibid.). For Hobbes, the only way to achieve this was to eliminate any metaphysical authority to which various factions could turn; 'to wipe the slate clean of all appeals to entities higher than civil authority' (ibid.). Once access to 'divine transcendence' has been closed off, the social contract can be enforced entirely by the Sovereign. Hobbes sees the social contract as an autonomous calculus reached 'abruptly and simultaneously by all the terrorized citizens who are seeking to liberate themselves from the state of nature', as well as from the vicissitudes of religious warfare (ibid.).

Boyle and Hobbes seem to stand on opposite ledges of an unbridgeable epistemological chasm – on one side the (constructed) autonomy of Nature or the 'Object pole', and on the other the autonomy of Society, or the 'Subject pole'. Effectively dividing up reality between them, into the objective (the non-human) and the discursive (the human), Boyle and Hobbes reject each other's methodology. Each insists on the 'purification' of his categories of knowledge and on the primacy of his construction: 'There is nothing but objective reality'/'there is nothing but political discourse'. Thus the founding tenets of the Modern Constitution are woven into a myth in which a knowable world can be achieved by 'a separation between the scientific power charged with representing things and the political power charged with representing subjects' (ibid.: 29).

What Boyle and Hobbes share, however, is a rationalist commitment to what Latour calls 'the Crossed-Out God', a tacit agreement that debates about knowledge cannot be solved by turning either to religious belief or to metaphysics. The Crossed-Out God, directly involved in neither Nature nor Society (but not exactly cut loose), lurks off in the distance, keeping a remote eye on a modernity that simultaneously denies his interventions and keeps him held in reserve as an 'impotent and sovereign judge':

> His transcendence distanced him infinitely, so that He disturbed neither the free play of Nature nor that of society, but the right was nevertheless reserved to appeal to that transcendence in case of conflict between the laws of Nature and those of Society. Modern men and women could thus be atheists even while remaining religious (ibid.: 33).

In this formulation, we can see how emergent 'modernity' sets the early stage for 'cynical idealism' by establishing a systematic way of believing and disbelieving simultaneously. With the Crossed-Out God remotely holding it all together, the moderns can begin their long march towards complete 'knowledge management'.

All of which would be tidy enough were it not for the fact that the total separation of the human and nonhuman realms poses a risk of interpretive paralysis, since in reality,

> everything happens in the middle, everything passes between the two, everything happens by way of mediation, translation

and networks; but this space does not exist, it has no place. It is the unthinkable, the unconscious of the moderns (ibid.: 37).

The very purification of categories that gives the moderns their authority *necessarily* generates hybrids: objects, say, that have a social function (commodities and fetishes, for example) and subjects who are treated as things or 'natural objects' (slaves or servants, for example). The more the subject/object poles are kept separate, the more quasi-subject and quasi-object hybrids proliferate. But the presence of these hybrids *must be denied*, since they threaten the integrity of the categories on which the Modern Constitution is based. This 'middle' space, which initially appears as an unbridgeable chasm, is in fact a vast terrain in which it is not always possible to tell what kind of creature, or text, one is dealing with. The inhabitants and products of this space are what the Modern Constitution relentlessly works either to identify (purify for one pole or the other) or to disavow.

If the discourse of modernity thereby limits the parameters of the 'knowable world' from the seventeenth-century forward, the discourse of rationalism has similarly limited the parameters of critical interpretation. The rationalist bias inherent in the 'Modern Constitution' is reproduced by both 'historicist' and 'materialist' readings of 'early modern' culture. To see how this works, let us briefly shift vocabularies. In her recent book *The Secret Life of Puppets*, Victoria Nelson traces the endurance of metaphysical thinking in secular western culture from Plato's *Republic* right up to current posthumanist cyborg fiction.[10] Cataloguing the persistence of 'irrational' cultural forms, she argues that western civilization is in fact constituted by the conflict between Platonic *gnosis* and the Aristotelian *episteme*. By the seventeenth and eighteenth centuries, the *episteme* reaches full ascendancy and all other ways of knowing are either discredited or back-burnered. Contemporary western consciousness is 'ruled by a strictly materialist episteme', which 'allows for only a mental or "subjective" inner world and a physical or "objective" outer world' (Nelson 2001: 29). The hegemony of materialism, however, has had an unfortunate side effect according to Nelson: 'some powerful fields of consciousness are opened up, but others are put off limits' (29). 'How', she asks, 'are we to explain this long love affair with realism, a mode of representation as artificial as any other, and no more "real"?' (79).[11]

The 'love affair with realism' permeates critical practice, and is without question the *ideological* foundation of literary historicism and materialism. The 'new historicism' was, and continues to be, a 'thoroughgoing rationalist' methodology that privileges the same formal conventions of plot and characterization as those of realist fiction. 'Thick description' – whether in the novels of Jane Austen or Henry James, the anthropology of Clifford Geertz, or the literary scholarship of Stephen Greenblatt or Robert Weimann – perpetuates the rationalist/empiricist fantasy of discursive control spun by the Modern Constitution. As Nelson points out about the empiricist bias,

> The worship of the fact, of solid documentary information, is a reality of mainstream American culture. The religion of the empirical carries with it the strong impulse to rationalize the irrational, to dethrone and 'manage' it (79–80).

The hegemony of historicism works by defining the limits of 'reality' in temporal terms, carving it into blocks or 'periods' (chronologically organized discursive laboratories) and then, in the critical equivalent of a Boylean experiment, proceeding to 'uncover' what its laboratory was always already designed to find. All of it performed for and verified by 'credible, trustworthy, well-to-do witnesses' – in other words, other historicists, which brings us to the relationship between the myth of modernity and the myth of 'historicity' as they have taken over the field, hand in glove, of Shakespeare criticism.

In *Shakespeare After Theory*, David Kastan argues that literary scholars 'must begin to respond to [literature's] significant challenges, not by producing more theory but more facts': facts of material production, facts of editorial work, facts of recorded reception.[12] Calling this approach 'the New Boredom', Kastan suggests that the time for theoretical fun is over – that we have outgrown the conceptual adolescence represented by 'theory' (like 'modernity,' a portmanteau word). Conceding with rueful fondness that the fancies of theory were necessary to critique and demystify naturalized categories of oppression such as race, class, and gender, Kastan asserts that the time has now come to return to the (presumably more grown-up) business of at least trying to uncover how things really were. Dealing with facts is boring, Kastan suggests (with faux regret), but somebody has to do away with the excesses of imagination that fuelled the rhapsodies of 'theory' in its heyday.

However, it is not so easy to turn a silk purse back into a sow's ear. Despite his ode to boredom, Kastan's own interpretive creativity will not let him sink to the level of boring himself, or others, with mere facts. Unwilling any longer simply to be 'lumped in' with the new historicists, and temperamentally unsuited to what he sees as the excesses of 'poststructuralism', Kastan urges us to produce facts for 'a definitive and usable historical knowledge'. Anticipating the criticism that he is merely returning to the positivism 'of an older, untheoretical historiography', he acknowledges that 'history can no longer pretend to recover and recount the past "as it actually was"' (Kastan 1999: 40).

This, however, is where things become confusing, and we begin to detect the trouble Kastan has negotiating between the subject and object 'poles' of modernity. On the one hand, he says 'we must produce more facts'. On the other, he says that 'we are not the producers of the past, we are only...producers of the meanings the past has for us' (ibid.: 41). Unable to separate out which version of rationalism he wishes to subscribe to – the Boylean or the Hobbesian – Kastan vacillates between them. One wonders how this could possibly produce 'a definitive' historical knowledge. Kastan's effort demonstrates how difficult it is to try to launch the 'next new thing' while still entangled in the same old epistemology:

> The past exists (for us now) as we construct it, but of course it existed independant of any of our representations; and that existence imposes an obligation upon and value for our constructions. To say that this existence cannot be apprehended except in mediated form...is only to say that it is past as well as to admit that history, like all other forms of human knowledge, is inevitably contingent but not obviously any more so or any more incapacitatingly than any other act of human understanding (41).

This revolving door of a statement is a textbook example of poststructuralism, one that wants to have its historical cake and keep its theory too. But instead of acknowledging that he is attempting to inhabit 'two realms of sensibility at the same time' (Nelson: 81) and how difficult it is to do so, Kastan sets up a straw man to deflect our attention away from his inconsistencies:

If we ignore the processes and practices by which the literary work is produced and read, we are left with an honorific and toothless formalism (Kastan: 41).

Formalism – the new historicist's default Godzilla – rears its ugly head again, this time 'honorific and toothless'. According to Kastan, if we do not study the production of the material text in its original historical context, we 'rob it of its actual ties to a social world of meaningful and multiple human agency' (41). Try as I might, I see only two alternatives being presented here: do what Kastan proposes or be a history-annihilating Robber. Kastan's suggestion that those concerned with the present are 'history annihilators' (ibid.: 17) is not only unfair but melodramatic.

I have singled Kastan out here not to criticize the intellectual work he does but because the first two chapters of *Shakespeare After Theory* are symptomatic of the 'collateral damage' produced by the Methodological SmackDown. Kastan knows that many theoretically sophisticated scholars are also knowledgeable about material production, and that many of us believe that the most relevant 'ties' a text can have to a 'social world of meaningful and multiple human agency' are ties to the present state of politics, law, economics, and mass culture. To read Shakespeare in this way is not to 'rob' him of anything but rather to borrow, on credit as it were, for present and future relevance. Of course it matters how people produced texts in the past. It matters just as much, if not more, how people read texts today.

If we recognize that the epistemologies we use have their own institutional politics, the objects of our study begin to look different. The artificial binaries of formalism versus materialism, 'theory' versus 'the archive', and 'presentism' versus 'historicism' are forced choices imposed by the larger artifice of the Modern Constitution. As long as literary scholars continue to uphold these divisions, we will support (whether we want to or not) the very myth of Enlightenment that in our various ways we purport to be deconstructing. A literary history more true to human experience would surely require us to be full citizens in *at least* two realms of sensibility at once, without elevating one at the expense of the other. And that would necessitate rethinking our relationship to time and to periodicity. Whenever we call ourselves 'early modernists' we implicitly accept the Moderns'

way of dividing up time, the Moderns' purification of categories
of experience into subject and object poles, and the concommi-
tant relegation of anything that does not conform to that division
to the status of disavowed hybrid.

What is the alternative? For one thing, we might rethink our
investment in our self-generated categories. For another, we
might try (just a little) to de-fetishize our own authority. In *Terrors
and Experts*, British essayist and psychoanalyst Adam Phillips has
said something about psychoanalysts that is equally appropriate
to literary critics:

> Psychoanalysis, as theory and practice, should not pretend to
> be important instead of keeping itself interesting (importance is
> a cure for nothing).... When psychoanalysts spend too much
> time with each other, they start believing in psychoanalysis.
> They begin to talk knowingly, like members of a religious cult.
> It is as if they have understood something. They forget, in
> other words, that they are only telling stories about stories; and
> that all stories are subject to an unknowable multiplicity of
> interpretations. The map becomes the ground beneath their
> feet; and maps are always a smaller ground (xvii).[13]

When historicists spend too much time with other historicists, they
too forget that they 'are only telling stories about stories'. We have
let the Modern Map become the ground underneath our feet; as a
result, the ground looks much smaller (and the terrain much more
uniform) than it really is. 'The Modern' has become our fetish.

Freud and Marx each defined the fetish as a substitutive thing – a
body part, an object, a reified commodity – that stands in for
disavowed knowledges and certain kinds of social relations. A fetish
provides a 'rigid designator', a point of fixation, for processes –
libidinal, cultural, intellectual – that are highly mobile and tend
not to lend themselves to rigorous verification. The key to understanding any fetish lies in the 'dreamwork', the rebus of affiliation,
that it allows. As Slavoj Žižek puts it, 'a fetish is the embodiment
of the Lie which enables us to sustain the unbearable truth'.[14] If
a fetish is a fragmentary embodiment of a larger ideological
fantasy, what is the 'unbearable truth' that the fetish of the modern
is designed to displace?

As our 'embodiment of the Lie', the category of 'the modern'
assures us that our epochs of 'irrationality' are behind us:

metaphysics, invisible hauntings, mysterious epiphenomena, chthonic attachments – surely these are the provinces of religious fanatics, terrorists, village idiots, people in third-world countries or the Balkans, and British soccer fans. The thought that what might *really* organize history are the still-swirling eddies of atavistic practices, unacknowledged primal drives and feelings, unspoken social 'contracts' based on 'tribal' alliances, and brain structures that are 6 million years old is simply unacceptable to anyone who wants to 'produce definitive historical knowledge'. If we are to be judged by our disavowals, maybe we really are 'modern' after all. But if we look more closely at the terrain we study, we can detect the ghostly hybrids that are doomed, for a certain term, to walk the earth until the map of the Moderns is burnt and purged away.

3
Dismember Me: Shakespeare, Paranoia, and the *Noir* World Order

> Whatever we may be, for better or for worse, we are thus
> initially and 'naturally' 'idiots of the family'.
> — Peter Sloterdijk[1]

> Be thy intents wicked or charitable,
> Thou com'st in such a questionable shape
> That I will speak to thee.
> — Hamlet[2]

I

The psychoanalytic coupling of Shakespeare's *Hamlet* and
Sophocles' *Oedipus* has a long and familiar trajectory, beginning
most notably with Freud's *Interpretation of Dreams* (1900) and
Ernest Jones' article on *Hamlet* and Oedipus (1910). Jacques
Lacan, in his 1958 seminar on desire, used *Hamlet* as his central
text. Lacan's refinement of Freud's theory of Oedipalism as a
sexual drive repositioned it instead as a fantasy that shapes the
subject's entrance into what he calls the 'symbolic' order. While
Lacan's reading of *Hamlet* permits more interpretive leeway than
Freud's, it similarly orbits around a family 'romance' of father,
mother, and son, remaining relatively unconcerned with the
political impact of that dynamic in the play. In general, stage as
well as film productions have long downplayed, and even eradi-
cated, the play's overarching political agenda, to such an extent

that a recent film critic finds Branagh's inclusion of the Fortin-bras 'subplot' in his 1996 film version an irritating distraction. Branagh's *Hamlet*, full of 'lots of superfluous stage business, such as the 'invasion' of Elsinore by the Norwegian troops led by Fortinbras, fails conclusively'.[3]

From the perspective of producing a 'tight' film, this view might make sense were it not for one inescapable fact: Fortin-bras' invasion is anything but superfluous. Shakespeare begins and ends the play with the problem of Norway's claims; and an Elizabethan audience worried about English succession in the last years of Elizabeth's life would have considered the threat to Denmark as a nation *at least* as important as Hamlet's state of mind. The failure of standard psychoanalysis, both Freudian and Lacanian, to speak to the play's political concerns has been a serious critical shortcoming, while the popularizing of Oedipal logic has overdetermined most film versions of the play, which (from Olivier's 1948 *Hamlet* forward) almost compulsively re-enact the tiresome triangle.

There is, however, a more recent version of Lacanian psycho-analysis that explicitly interweaves traumas of individual subjec-tivity and state politics. To marshal its interpretive insights for *Hamlet*, we need to take a brief detour through the genre of detective fiction. In *Enjoy Your Symptom: Jacques Lacan In Hollywood and Out*, Slavoj Žižek makes an intriguing link between a change that occurs in modern detective fiction and the emergence of film *noir*. In a chapter entitled 'Why are there always two Fathers?' Žižek defines the difference between the 'classical' (logic-and-deduction) detective novel and the 'hard-boiled novel' largely as a change in the subjective universe of the detective:

> The logic-and-deduction novel still relies on the consistent big Other: the moment, at the novel's end, when the flow of events is integrated into the symbolic universe, narrativized, told in the form of a linear story (the last pages of the novel when, upon identifying the murderer, the detective reconstructs the true course of events), brings about an effect of pacification, order and consistency are reinstated, whereas the noir universe is characterized by a radical split, a kind of structural imbalance, as to the possibility of narrativization: the integration of the subject's position into the field of the big

Other, the narrativization of his fate, becomes possible only when the subject is in a sense already dead, although still alive, when the 'game is already over,' in short: when the subject finds himself at the place baptized by Lacan 'the in-between-two-deaths'. [*l'entre-deux-morts*][4]

This Big Other, as Lacan defines it in his second *Seminar*, is that fantasmatic entity that does not exist separately from the subject but nonetheless calls the subject into 'the being of the other', into 'identification' within the symbolic order.[5] It is that phantom to whom we all address the constitutive question 'Che Vuoi?' or, What is it that you want of me? Purely structural – that is to say, devoid of any particular content – the Big Other is effective only when misrecognized as an essential 'being' that guarantees the integrity of subjective and social life. In patriarchal culture, the place of the Big Other may be occupied by God, King, Pope, Lord, Father – placeholders who quilt a paternal allegory over an antagonistic social formation and call things to order and account within it.[6] Such interpellations, however, can only operate successfully if the paternal metaphor remains neutral, or 'in the background', as Žižek puts it. By holding itself 'in reserve,' the Big Other allows the subject to imagine a site – always 'elsewhere' – of absolute knowledge, unblemished authority, and rational control that organizes the subject's narrative integration into the social order, assigning him (or her) a place in the story.

Against this 'neutral' paradigm, Žižek aligns the emergence of the *Noir* universe with a disturbance in the field of the Big Other, one that makes the mandates of identification ambiguous. This disturbance is brought about by the revelation of another father, a figure who emerges as 'the obscene, uncanny shadowy double of the Name of the Father':

> Instead of the traditional father – guarantor of the rule of Law, i.e., the father who exerts his power as fundamentally *absent*, whose fundamental feature is not an open display of power but the threat of potential power – we obtain an excessively *present* father, who, as such, cannot be reduced to the bearer of a symbolic function.[7]

Whereas the classical (logic-and-deduction) detective may be worldly wise and even cynical (Chandler's Philip Marlowe, for example), he still sustains belief in the abstraction called 'Law', and therefore can sustain *our* identification with *his* identification with the 'paternal metaphor'. The hard-boiled detective, however (represented by a figure such as Hammett's Ned Beaumont), is a kind of blank page, offering the reader no stable point of affective entry because his universe is organized according to a different logic: the logic of *Noir*. At the origins of *Noir*, Žižek points out, is the 'humiliated Father', 'the paranoiac Other', a figure who has sustained irreparable damage to his integrity and can no longer function as symbolic guarantor of all the institutions established in 'his' name.[8] The nature of this 'mutation in the paternal figure' is one of prurient pleasure, the obscene enjoyment that Lacan claims always underwrites paternal law. This second father – the obscene father – is first and foremost a 'father-who-knows', and whose knowledge specifically is of the licentiousness that Law must disavow in order to maintain its unquestionable shape.[9]

The splitting of detective fiction into two genres – classical and *noir* – makes the reader/audience choose between contradictory forms of symbolic authority. The first offers a pragmatic or rationalist ethos in which what matters most is the fact that a crime has been committed and a law breached, a situation which requires only detection and punishment in order to set things right. The latter offers a *paranoiac* ethos in which the fact of a particular crime is not only insufficient to explain what has really gone wrong, but draws attention to a more pervasive social problem.

Although Žižek suggests that the elements of classical and *noir* detective fictions are mutually incompatible (presumably because, like oil and water, they have incommensurable properties), both forms descend from a single, earlier genre: the revenge tragedy, a form of drama in which a revenger/'detective' discovers that a crime has been committed (usually, but not always, against a father figure), uncovers the details, and sets out to bring the offender to justice. The nature of that justice may be harsh – the Law of the Father to which the classical revenger subscribes does not yet have to hide its foundational violence behind the Enlightenment mask of disinterestedness. But in revenge tragedy (as in classical detective fiction), the authority of the paternal metaphor remains intact regardless of the violence loosed in its name, for it is underwritten by the patriarchal power encoded in every aspect of ancient and early modern life. The classical revenge play – whether Greek or Roman revenge tragedy, Heywood's translations of Senecan tragedy, or early modern translations of the *Orestes* – tends to offer a 'logic-and-deduction' rationale that, no matter how violent or passionate, is ultimately about restoring an ethical system based on structural checks and balances. Most importantly, Renaissance revengers (despite the contradictions of Christian philosophy) are expected in the last instance to cease whining and get the job done.

The play that has for centuries most famously represented the revenge tragedy 'tradition' is, of course, Shakespeare's *Hamlet*, which, in terms of its popular or mass cultural reception, has long been regarded as *the classic* Renaissance revenge play. The play clearly inherits, deploys, and satirizes certain elements of Senecan and classical tragedy. At the same time, *Hamlet* has been read – through centuries of critical reception at least – as 'breaking' with that tradition – indeed, as breaking with an already established tradition of specifically *English* revenge tragedy. Since among extant English plays that precede *Hamlet* (not including *Gorboduc*) there is only one – Kyd's *Spanish Tragedy* – that fits into the 'subgenre' we call revenge tragedy, we are presented with an intriguing paradox.

Did Shakespeare mean the play to depart from a 'logic-and-deduction' formula that he presumed already existed for his audience? Or was he attempting something more radical: to launch, and simultaneously critique, a 'logic-and-deduction' tradition precisely by staging an epistemological 'break' with it?[10] Although there are few 'logic-and-deduction' revengers running around on the Renaissance stage before Shakespeare's *Hamlet* appears, the play *acts as if there are*, constructs the subjectivity of its protagonist as if there are, and presumes an audience – ingenuously or disingenuously – that must consent (to paraphrase Frank Kermode) to 'the sense of a tradition' in order to identify with the protagonist.

Given the impossibility of determining exactly what audience expectations would have been with regard to an already-existing revenge *ethos*, it would be more accurate to say that the play deliberately generates a *tradition-effect* by counterposing Hamlet against other sons *within* the play (Fortinbras, Laertes, and in 'the Mousetrap', Lucianus) who do conform to a 'logic-and-deduction' model. At once prototype *and* changeling, Shakespeare's *Hamlet* stages exactly the kind of epistemological mortification that necessarily vexes *any* tradition based on the unquestioned authority of patriarchal law. The history of the play's construction as a 'classic' revenge tragedy within a 'tradition' – both in terms of critical and popular reception – reproduces the dilemma that Hamlet is forced to face within the play itself: Where do we locate the *origin* of a larger problem that needs to be redressed? For in asking whether it is better to suffer the requirements of a paternal mandate to revenge a crime, or to take no arms against a more pervasive sea of troubles, Hamlet is asking no less a question than what kind of detective he is to be or not to be.

If we accept Žižek's description of the *noir* universe, then we must conclude that *Hamlet* – and not Hammett – offers the first fully *noir* text in western literature, and prince Hamlet the first *noir* detective. Or rather, the first *noir* revenger. Situating a plot-driven classical revenge tragedy within the recursive circularity and ethical indeterminacy that characterize *noir*, Shakespeare's *Hamlet* is modernity's inaugural paranoid text.[11] By 'paranoid', however, I do not mean an individual pathology in which someone imagines conspiracies or has delusions of persecution, but rather, paranoid in the Greek sense of 'overknowing', of a surplus knowledge that leads, paradoxically, not to discovery but to undecidability. In the *noir* universe, the paranoid is a man who always already 'knows too much' about what is really going on. The *noir* detective is less concerned with historical events – with what *happened* – than he is with ontologies – with the way things *are*. If the classical detective wants 'just the facts', for the *noir* detective the 'facts' are always less relevant than the sinister effects of a reality that acquires paranoid dimensions precisely the more one learns about the 'facts'.

In Shakespeare's *Hamlet*, the ghost is a 'father who knows', and whose knowledge threatens the status of the symbolic mandate he imposes upon his son. The content of this knowledge consists not only of the 'harrowing' secrets of his purgatorial prison house, but more disturbingly, of his 'enjoyment' of the 'blossoms of his sin', for which, he tells Hamlet, he is 'confined to fast in fires, / Till the foul crimes done in my days of nature / Are burnt and purged away' (1.5.10–12). At once delivering the injunction to 'revenge his foul and unnatural murder' and revealing his own sinister 'double', the ghost commands Hamlet to 'Remember me' even as he makes the task impossible, delivering the mandate from a corrupted and compromised position that can scarcely lay claim to moral authority. 'This', Žižek argues, 'is what is ulti- mately at stake in the *noir* universe: the failure of the paternal metaphor... the emergence of the obscene father who supplants the father living up to his symbolic function'.[12]

The ghost's disclosure reveals a figure hopelessly at odds with the 'Hyperion' Hamlet wishes to champion. Sensing an exces- sively obscene presence in the environment before he even encounters the ghost, Hamlet is casting about for a local habita- tion, a concrete cause. His ontological despair, already legible in his withdrawal from the 'stale, flat and unprofitable... uses of this world', signals his inability to integrate himself in the symbolic order, into the 'intersubjective, "public"... space' that gives the subject his 'ideal ego, the place from which he can see himself as someone "who belongs"'.[13] Hamlet attempts to respond as a classical revenger, to gather facts in 'logic-and- deduction' style. But the more he seeks to confirm the knowledge *he already has* of Claudius's guilt, the more he is paralyzed by the gravitational pull of a different crime scene. For when the ghost reveals the lurid details of his murder, he also makes 'excessively present' to his son's imagination images of his own lascivious body, taken in postprandial concupiscence, 'grossly full of bread', and 'barked about... with a vile and loathsome crust.' Hamlet's subsequent disavowal of this other 'second' father fuels his compulsive commitment to a 'logic-and-deduction' style that the ghost's narrative should have rendered unnecessary.

In other words, Hamlet now has 'the facts', at least insofar as he knows that Claudius has committed regicide, fratricide, usur- pation, and 'damned incest'. But Hamlet cannot act on this knowledge because action is impossible in a *noir* universe where what is at stake is not a local crime but rather, the very status of the paternal logos itself. Unable to assume the symbolic exist- ence that paternal identification confers, but not yet physically dead, Hamlet (like the *noir* detective) finds himself *l'entre-deux- morts*, in the place 'between two deaths'. Incapable of finding his place in the story, Hamlet literally 'lacks advancement'. 'The time is out of joint', he says, 'O cursed spite, / That ever I was born to set it right' (1.5.196–7). The shift from the 'classical' to the *noir* universe triggers a vertiginous jolt out of sequential time and into synchronic space. Within this miasma, in which the 'questionable shape' of the ghost looms so large as to eclipse the passage of time, the whole meaning of 'solving a crime' changes.

As much as Hamlet detests his uncle, Claudius offers a temporary relief from the shock of discovering that his late father was capable of 'foul crimes'. However, like all supplements, Claudius cannot contain everything he is supposed to 'stand for'. There must be other sites of displacement. As Žižek points out,

> The failure of the paternal metaphor renders impossible a viable, temperate relation with a woman; as a result the woman finds herself occupying the impossible space of the traumatic Thing. The femme fatale is nothing but a lure whose fascinating presence masks the true traumatic axis of the noir universe, the relationship to the obscene father, ie, the default of the paternal metaphor... The crucial point not to be missed here is that the femme fatale and the obscene-knowing father cannot appear simultaneously within the same narrative space.[14]

As long as the real obscene father hovers unacknowledged in the *noir* background, Gertrude, as well as Ophelia, can take on for Hamlet the function of 'traumatic Thing'. With a circuit of disavowal which runs from the obscene father to Claudius to Gertrude to Ophelia to Gertrude and finally back to Claudius, we see Hamlet's desperate efforts to construct himself as a classical revenger in a world where corruption, crime, licentiousness, and decay can be seen everywhere *but* in the place of the Father.

For in Shakespeare's play, the King may be a thing that demands; but the King must not be a thing that *enjoys*. If he is, he becomes a different kind of thing, something that produces *noir* paranoia because his authority is no longer purified by disinterestedness. It is, therefore, no accident that in Shakespeare's play, the only cure for the *noir* must come from outside the given social formation. Fortinbras (a true 'logic-and-deduction' type) enters only after the occupants of the *noir* universe are all dead. By presenting us in *Hamlet* with 'two-fathers' in one king, Shakespeare makes it impossible to separate familial from national corruption. In Shakespeare's world, contamination of paternal authority leads directly to the death of the state.

II

A letter always reaches its destination.

– Jacques Lacan

A letter sometimes (never) doesn't reach its destination.

– Jacques Derrida[15]

If Shakespeare's *Hamlet* maps out the social and subjective indeterminacies of *noir* paranoia long before Ned Beaumont is even a gleam in Dashiell Hammett's eye, Franco Zeffirelli's 1990 film version attempts to return the play to the world of classical revenge, plucking out the heart of the play's mystery by restoring the father to his 'proper' place through the classical psychoanalytic logic of Oedipus. The casting of the film initiates the Oedipal 'feint' before its action even begins by performing what Barbara Klinger has called the 'inferential walk'.[16] Urging the need to include all of a film's 'digressive' production processes in our interpretation of its significance as a cultural product, Klinger argues that 'films circulate as products, not in a semantic vacuum, but in a mass cultural environment teeming with related commercial significations'. This 'adjacent territory', as Klinger calls it, is constituted by epiphenomena – promotion, advertisements, star interviews, and spin-off product lines – which 'create not only a commercial life-support system for a film, but also a socially meaningful network of relations around it which enter into reception' (1991: 117–34).

The territory also includes what I would call the cultural logic of commodity casting: celebrities who already exist in the culture as signifying products, beyond the formal boundaries of their respective 'texts'. This is how commodity casting generates the 'inferential walk' (a term Klinger borrows from Umberto Eco's semiotic theory of intertextuality). According to Eco, such 'walks' occur when 'the reader digresses to gather the intertextual support necessary to decipher a moment within the narrative' (Klinger 1991: 130). The 'moment' that needs deciphering within the narrative of Zeffirelli's *Hamlet* is the film's opening scene in the family tomb, in which Oedipus is quite literally encrypted. With ham-fisted manipulation, Zeffirelli thrusts us into the family romance by banking on the audience's 'inferences' about the stars' prior filmic incarnations.

Mel Gibson, already familiar to cult audiences as *Mad Max* and more famously, to mass audiences, as *Lethal Weapon*, has built a career playing characters who hath been made mad by marriages. In *Road Warrior* he is a post-nuclear apocalypse policeman out to revenge the murder of his wife. In the *Lethal Weapon* series, he plays yet another policeman – Sgt. Riggs – who has lost his wife to murder. He is considered 'mad' because his police methods suggest a 'fatal attraction' to suicide. By the time Gibson makes it into Zeffirelli's *Hamlet*, he is used to playing characters who curse spite for bearing him to set things right.[17] And Glenn Close's roles, first as the 'radiant angel' mother in *The World According to Garp, The Natural,* and *The Big Chill,* and then as the sexual predator Alex in *Fatal Attraction,* more than ensure her 'inferential walk' to Elsinore as Gertrude. Zeffirelli's choice of actors to play the roles of Hamlet and Gertrude effects a cinematic intertextuality that guarantees that the audience will see through the lens of what Gilles Deleuze and Felix Guattari have called 'holy familialism'.[18]

Deleuze and Guattari argue that the psychoanalytic implementation of the Oedipal triangle – 'daddy-mommy-me' – has generated a dogma that has become tantamount to a kind of 'imperialism', one in which every form of cultural desire can, and must for the logic of capitalism to work, be forced into a structure that depends simultaneously on desire and renunciation. By telling us what it is 'we all really want', and then insisting that we renounce it for a simulacrum that will forever be 'not it', psychoanalysis underwrites late capitalism by guaranteeing the perpetual inadequacy of the very 'substitutive' or fetishistic objects it offers. Thus the desiring subject, in the repetition-compulsion that capitalist production depends upon, is forever seeking to find what it is he 'really wants' while remaining permanently barred from the possibility of ever attaining it.

This is the brand of Oedipalism that Zeffirelli's *Hamlet* taps into. Through the cultural logic of commodity casting, his film propagates the particular form of 'desiring production' that most successfully underwrites late capitalism: one in which we are all 'initially and "naturally" idiots of the family'.[19] To begin with, Zeffirelli cuts the play's crucial opening scene, eliminating Marcellus's question about why 'the strict and most observant watch / So nightly toils the subject of the land', and Horatio's consequent answer about Fortinbras and the threat of war. In fact, Fortinbras drops out of Zeffirelli's version altogether. The 'action', therefore, will portend not 'strange eruption [s] to [the] state' (1.1.69), but merely strange eruptions in the family.

While Shakespeare's play opens in murky and amorphous darkness, with a sentinel asking the classic paranoid question – 'Who's there?' – Zeffirelli's film begins with a scene not in the play at all, one almost orificial in its constriction, within a womblike sepulchur, of Hamlet, Claudius, and Gertrude around the open casket of the dead King. The first words in the film are spoken quietly by Claudius directly to the young prince, as all three stand contemplating the corpse: 'Hamlet, think of us as of a father' (1.2.64). There is no court in Zeffirelli's version to witness Claudius's words, no sense that they are being 'performed' for political reasons. The effect of such 'privatizing' is to render the scene claustrophobically Oedipal, with Claudius (played by a sanguine and overfed Alan Bates) looming as the 'excessively present' obscene father.

In Shakespeare's play we see the King only as ghost, never as corpse. However, by 'producing the body' of the dead King in the casket, Zeffirelli himself operates like a classical detective.[20] As Žižek has pointed out about the function of the corpse in detective fiction, 'the corpse as object works to bind a group of individuals together: the corpse constitutes them as a group'. In Zeffirelli's film, the corpse constitutes a nuclear family from Hell, efficiently scored by Claudius's 'like-a-Father' refrain. Although Hamlet will, much later in the film, encounter the ghost on the battlements, the effect here of displaying the corpse is neatly to separate the gross materiality of the king from its spectral remainder. While in the play we first encounter the ghost upright in his 'fair and warlike form' (1.1.47), terrifyingly mobile and dressed in armor 'cap-a-pie', in Zeffirelli we get the father first as mere 'matter' – horizontal and inert – a body without desire, without any trace of 'vile and loathsome crust', and clearly incapable of 'foul crimes'. Zeffirelli cinematically redistributes the 'two fathers' – which in the *noir* are embodied in one figure – between the ghost, who becomes the 'in reserve', withdrawn father, guarantor of paternal law, and Claudius, who becomes the 'obscene-knowing' father.[21]

By cleaning up the king's body and downloading the 'other' father into Claudius, Zeffirelli offers Oedipus as the logic-and-deduction answer to what in Shakespeare's play is a *noir* question. In Zeffirelli's version, it is Claudius who looks 'grossly full of bread' and not the ghost (played, with Thomas More-like probity, by Paul Scofied), who appears wan, gaunt, and elderly. Taking Hamlet's words literally – 'my father, in his habit as he lived' (130) – Zeffirelli's ghost is dressed austerely in a monk's habit. The 'questionable shape' of the ghost in Shakespeare's play becomes in Zeffirelli's film the unquestionable shape of Claudius's desire, as he – and not the late king – is assigned the role of 'Master of Enjoyment'.

In Shakespeare's play, Claudius functions as Hamlet's *identified* symptom – the figure in whom unseemly pleasures and 'foul crimes' can be encountered, thereby leaving intact the pristine perfection of the father. With his bluntly literal imagination, Zeffirelli falls for Shakespeare's own Oedipal feint, taking it for the truth of Hamlet's desire by crudely parading it in vaudevillian winks, heated glances, passionate kisses and lubricious encounters between Gibson's Hamlet and Close's Gertrude.

Encouraged by Zeffirelli to cast our lot with the lad, we too can direct our loathing towards a corrupt Claudius because, while he may be lewd, he does not inspire paranoia since (after all) he does not know anything that *we* do not know. His obscenity – predicated on the readily comprehensible and ultimately banal motivations of ambition, lust, and envy – *can* be contained within the confines of his overblown body. Neither spectral nor *noir*, he does not threaten the integrity of the symbolic order because we know what *his* enjoyment is about. We can attribute it, as Hamlet does, to a corrupt individual, leaving the paternal metaphor, the symbolic order, and, by extension, the state respectfully intact. Reassuring the audience by getting us to 'enjoy' Hamlet's symptom as our own, Zeffirelli instructs us about what everyone in the play 'really' wants. By substituting Oedipal constraints for the riskier indeterminacies of *Noir*, Zeffirelli bypasses the paranoia induced precisely when Oedipus *fails* to overdetermine the subject positions of its 'members'. As Deleuze and Guattari have put it,

> Oedipus is... only the represented, insofar as it is induced by repression. Repression cannot act without displacing desire, without giving rise to a *consequent desire*, all ready, all warm for

punishment, and without putting this desire in the place of the *antecedent desire* on which repression comes to bear in principle or in reality ['Ah, so *that's* what it was!'].[22]

In Shakespeare's play, Hamlet's 'consequent desire', 'all ready, all warm for punishment', is to kill Claudius and get him out of his mother's bed. But his 'antecedent desire', repressed under the *sign* of Oedipus, is to ask the one question that sits, unenunciated but brooding, over the vast abyss: What, exactly, *were* those 'foul crimes' committed in your days of nature? *What did Daddy do?*

Looking for lack in all the wrong places, Zeffirelli sutures what Shakespeare's play has rent asunder, 'curing' the paranoia of *Noir* with the more familiar discomforts of Oedipus, which can themselves be cured by returning subjects to their proper relation to 'desiring production'. There is no hostile takeover of the state at the end of Zeffirelli's film; and while his Hamlet must of course die, at least he dies as an 'orthopsychic subject' – straightened out by his acceptance of what it was he 'really wanted'.[23]

III

Thus Zeffirelli's *Hamlet* reinstalls the father at the top of a hierarchy that guarantees the stability of the paternal metaphor and the unquestionable nature of paternal Law. However, there is another, comedic version of *Hamlet* that, like Zeffirelli's, was also released in 1990. Neither Oedipal nor *Noir*, Steve Martin's *LA Story* does not take the name of Shakespeare's play; but it remains (arguably) the most 'postmodern' version of *Hamlet* undertaken on film to date. *LA Story* begins with the edited words of another Shakespearean father, John of Gaunt (from *King Richard II*), who is soon to join the ranks of the dead:

> This royal throne of kings, this sceptred isle,
> This earth of majesty, this seat of Mars,
> This other Eden, demi-paradise,
> This happy breed of men, this little world,
> This precious stone set in the silver sea,
> This blessed plot, this earth, this realm, this
> Los Angeles.

Narrated against the backdrop of a 'fitness' park, these lines cele-brate a Utopian Los Angeles that is, in its white luminosity, the opposite of a rank and rotten Denmark. In *LA Story*, the lines are 'imported' while their site of enunciation (a dying father predicting disaster for the state) is jettisoned. The protagonist of the film, Martin's character Harris K. Telemacher, is not bothered by parents: he has no father and we never see or hear his mother. Even without the burden of parents, however, Harris finds himself brooding over his condition. In one of his many 'soliloquies', he tells us: 'I was deeply unhappy, but I didn't know it because I was so happy all the time.' Like Hamlet, Harris 'lacks advancement'. Overeducated and philosophically inclined (he has a Ph.D. in 'Arts and Humanities'), he works as a television weatherman, reporting the 'wacky weekend weather'. Humiliated by the need to put on an 'antic disposition' to keep ratings up, his life, he says (poaching from *Macbeth*), is 'a tale told by an idiot, full of sound and fury, signifying nothing'.

In other words, Harris suffers from the postmodern equivalent of Hamlet's ontological despair: he is, he writes in boldface on his living-room window, '**Bored Beyond Belief**'. One evening, as he drives home from yet another superficial social event, his car stalls on the side of the freeway. As he checks under the hood, he is 'hailed' by a huge electronic signpost that normally broadcasts traffic conditions:

Sign:	Hiya.
	I said HIYA
	RU OK
Harris:	Who are you?
Sign:	I'm a signpost
Harris:	Why are you talking to me?
Sign:	I see people in trouble and I stop them
	LA wants 2 help U
	U will know what 2 do when you unscramble
	HOW DADDY IS DOING
	(its a riddle)
Harris:	Whose Daddy? Who's Daddy?

Like Hamlet, Harris knows he has been given a 'wakeup call' to change his life; but he is unable to make any sense out of the signpost's riddle because he *literally cannot remember* Daddy ('Who is Daddy?').

Later in the film, in an almost verbatim replay of the gravedigger's scene, the *Hamlet* motif openly emerges to remind Harris (and us) that there is something to be, or not to be, remembered. Harris and his new love Sarah are strolling through a cemetery, where they happen upon a gravedigger. Hard upon an exchange of questions and answers that come (with slight modernizing) from *Hamlet* 5.1, the gravedigger produces a Yorick-like skull. Harris asks whose grave it is, and the gravedigger tells him, 'some guy named Blunderman'. 'Blunderman', Harris muses – 'I knew him. A funny guy.' Sarah quickly and gamely enters into the *Hamlet* scenario: 'where be thy gibes now?' she says, playing Horatio to Harris's Hamlet.

Sarah's ability to 'remember' the play at this moment allows Harris to realize that he is in love with her.[24] At the end of the film, after all comedic obstacles to their love have been 'magically' removed, they are irresistibly drawn back to the signpost, for its riddle remains to be solved. While Harris is still perplexed, Sarah takes one look at 'How Daddy is Doing' and recognizes it as a word scramble, or 'jumble'. She rearranges the order of the letters until a new 'message' appears: 'I know what it is', she declares, 'it's Sing Doo Wah Diddy'.

Reversing the ordinary logic of a 'jumble', which usually begins with a nonsense statement that 'unscrambles' into sense, solving this riddle literally means making nonsense of the question of how Daddy is doing. Indeed, it means dissolving Daddy altogether, not only at the level of the signified ('Whose Daddy? Who is Daddy?'), but at the level of the signifier: Daddy becomes Diddy. 'Hailed' by an injunction from a sign that is ghostly yet no ghost, Harris is interpellated by a Big Other that is entirely benevolent: 'LA Wants 2 Help U.' While it poses a question about the father, it is neither from nor of the Father, since the question is never meant to be answered. In this way, Hamlet's ontological dilemma – how to re-assemble a particular father who is in fact two fathers, one a Hyperion and the other a Satyr – becomes in Steve Martin's postmodern version, a categorical dilemma (who is Daddy?) solved by eliminating the paternal signifier altogether.

'Remember me' becomes 'Dismember me', as the film celebrates a postmodern subjectivity that requires nothing from the father, and more importantly, the father requires nothing from

the subject because he is no longer there. Neither *noir* nor classical, spectral nor Oedipal, this Big Other makes no demands
(apart from, that is, the signpost's demand for a HUG). In *LA
Story*, Harris is not faced with what kind of detective to be
because if Daddy is Diddy he need not ask either what did
Daddy do or how Daddy is doing. The Oedipal 'logic-and-
deduction' approach that characterizes Zeffirelli's 'cure' of *Hamlet*
is in *LA Story* irrelevant because there is nothing to 'find out' and
no one to find it out about. Harris himself seems baffled by it all
at the end, as he says to the signpost: 'Sing doo wah Diddy?
That's the mystery of the ages?' The signpost replies, 'There are
more things under heaven and earth, Harris, than are dreamt of
in your philosophy.'

Beginning with the elegiac words of a dying father, *LA Story*
ends, like Shakespeare's John of Gaunt, by 'playing nicely with
the name'. The solution to the signpost's riddle implies that the
symbolic order itself is based on nonsense: on an arbitrary imposition of power that has no 'essential' or 'original' foundation.
This elimination of what Terence Hawkes has called 'paternal
overkill'[25] has several advantages, not the least of which is that it
permits a fantasy of romantic love to triumph. While Hamlet's
disavowal of his own father launches a great chain of displacement that leads to Ophelia's death, in *LA Story* Harris gets to
have his Ophelia and keep her too. Unlike the *noir* universe, in
which 'the failure of the paternal metaphor...renders impossi-
ible a viable, temperate relation with a woman', in *LA Story*'s
version of *Hamlet* we have not paternal failure but foreclosure;
consequently romantic love occludes not only the crisis of
Oedipus but the crisis of the state.

With breezy *savoir faire*, *LA Story* manages to achieve the
impossible: a version of *Hamlet* that eliminates familial, intergenerational, and national politics while rescuing Hamlet and
Ophelia for a happy ending. In its complete translation of *noir*
into *blanc*, *LA Story* is remarkably instructive about politics at the
turn of the millennium: a textbook example of fetishistic disavowal. It is no accident that the racial and socio-economic world
represented in film is almost entirely white and upper-middle
class. Its fiction of a Los Angeles blissfully united by singing 'doo
wah diddy' is also one of a world without the need for police.
There is no homelessness in the film, no poverty, no racial

conflict, and no one is accountable to any Law other than that, perhaps, of the fascist *Maitre d'* of the restaurant *L'Idiot*, who insists on seeing your bank statement before he will take your dinner reservation; and crime – stripped of its deadly reality – seamlessly converges with the middle-class 'lifestyle' as customers and muggers line up at the Ready Teller Machine – 'Hi, I'm Bob, I'll be your robber tonight.'

The real Los Angeles, however, occupies the 'space off', to use Teresa de Lauretis's term, of *LA Story*: what the film points to, by excluding, just beyond its cinematic frame.[26] Its vision of a white, prosperous Los Angeles depends on a denial of what is taking place offscreen (as all cities that promote 'theme park' images, whether Los Angeles, or London, or New Orleans, depend on such denials). However 'light' Martin's version of *Hamlet* may seem, its relief is merely a bulwark against the racial and class conflicts that in the 1990s were making Los Angeles, and American culture more generally, a pressure cooker ready to explode. The film was released virtually on the eve of the Rodney King beating.[27] As Žižek puts it, 'we fear the policeman insofar as he is not just himself…that is to say, insofar as he is experienced as the stand in for the big Other, for the social order'.[28]

The moment that the 'stand ins' for the Big Other reveal their enjoyment is the moment that we enter the *noir* universe. The *noir* detective learns to his disgust that the local crimes he uncovers originate in the very law that authorizes his actions: that the Name of the Father covers over a metastatic corruption that reproduces its crimes at precisely the same moment that it reproduces its authority. In Shakespeare's *Hamlet*, every 'idiot of the family' is also an idiot of the state. If it is true that there are always two fathers, then the noir paranoid is *always* right.

4
We Were Never Early Modern

> The crisis in historicity now dictates a return, in a new way,
> to the question of temporal organization in general in the post-
> modern force field, and indeed, to the problem of the form
> that time, temporality, and the syntagmatic will be able to take
> in a culture increasingly dominated by space and spatial logic.
> – Fredric Jameson (1991)

At a time when contemporary culture is undergoing what
Fredric Jameson has called 'the crisis of historicity', Shakespeare
has never been more popular.[1] At first glance this may seem
paradoxical, since most people probably feel when they see
something 'Shakespearean' that they are having an encounter
with 'History'. Jameson is right that there is a 'crisis' of some
kind with regard to 'historicity'; but it does not consist of a lack of
interest in 'the historical'. Mass culture is aswarm with 'histories',
real and imagined. By 'the historical' however, I do not mean
historiography as the art of writing events into that reified form
we call history, but rather, a particular 'structure of feeling': a
certain *je ne sais quoi* which lets us feel as if we are still living in a
world marked by the passage of *meaningful* time. To understand
Shakespeare's remarkable cachet at the turn of the millennium,
we should pay attention to what signifies 'historicity' beyond
academia. For whatever else Shakespeare may represent, in
mass culture he has become a stand-in for 'History itself'.

This version of history is, however, increasingly apparitional,
increasingly resistant to the demands of 'temporal organization'.

An apparitional Shakespeare is entirely appropriate in a culture that seeks 'the historical' not in narrative but in 'appearances' – in the figures of famous persons themselves. A brief look at the 1992 film *Bill and Ted's Excellent Adventure* easily demonstrates this phenomenon. Bill and Ted are two middle-class seniors in Southern California, on the verge of flunking out of high school. Unless they can present a successful history project, Bill and Ted will not graduate with their class. Faced with this 'most heinous' possibility and knowing nothing about history, Bill and Ted manage to attract the help of faux-Olympian powers who equip them with a time machine in the form of a telephone booth (complete with a dialing-for-destinies directory).

All Bill and Ted have to do is let their fingers do the walking through the phone book of history: the machine carries them back to different periods and places, to the sides of the famous figures they ring up. Due to serious time constraints and limited attention spans, Bill and Ted decide that rather than learn about history step by step chronologically, they will simply bring some historical 'dudes' back to the future with them, to appear on the high school stage as 'themselves', literally embodying History. Since their curriculum requires 'coverage', Bill and Ted round up Socrates, Genghis Khan, Billy the Kid, Napoleon, Joan of Arc, Beethoven, Freud, and Lincoln. At the film's end, the simultaneous presence of these figures in a musical extravaganza on the auditorium stage perfectly exemplifies postmodernist history as pastiche: the way in which contemporary mass culture substitutes fantasies of hyper-real presence – what Baudrillard calls *pataphysics*, a 'science of imaginary solutions' (1993: 149) – for the temporal organizations which produce more traditional narratives of history.

However, while Bill and Ted seem to choose their historical figures capriciously (and one would not want to lean too hard on whatever crude principle of selection guides them), no choice that depends on instant name recognition can ever truly be random. No matter how disjointed they may appear, these figures stand, in the 'science of imaginary solutions' respectively, for Wisdom (Socrates), Warrior Culture (Genghis Khan), the Wild West (Billy the Kid), Empire (Napoleon), Religious Zeal (Joan of Arc), Musical Genius (Beethoven), Modern Neurosis (Freud), and Freedom from Slavery (Lincoln). Apart from two token gestures towards multiculturalism (Genghis Khan) and gender (Joan of Arc), these historical figures signify (reductively to be sure) western civilization's simplistic binary divisions of history into a dialectic between authoritarian conservativism on the one hand and innovative 'radicalism' on the other. Consequently, despite its pretensions to postmodern self-irony, the film's cultural intertext is neither postmodern nor post-historicist. Legible within the film, beneath the rubble of its banality, is an embrace of a *kind* of history.

Of course Bill and Ted make a major mistake by neglecting to collect Shakespeare who, had he been on board, no doubt would have appeared on stage holding a skull and reciting Hamlet's 'to be or not to be' speech. For 'to be or not to be' is the question at the root of any history. It is therefore no accident (despite Bill and Ted's oversight) that *Hamlet* is the play to which contemporary culture most frequently returns. Prince Hamlet has come to stand for the dilemma of historicity itself. The play raises the hoary spectres that always haunt positivist narratives, and reveals that the 'crisis of historicity' – the politics of how stories achieve or lack advancement – has a much longer trajectory than is dreamt of in Jameson's philosophy.

At stake are two kinds of historical production: one narrative and the other apparitional, each of which generates different experiences of time and incompatible representations of subjectivity. Within a Lacanian framework, the subject of narrative time is a dead letter, a reified historical figure who only exists in what Bruno Latour calls 'calendar time'. Calendar time 'situate[s] events with respect to a regulated series of dates'. There is, however, another kind of time that 'situates the same events with respect to their intensity' (1993: 68). *To situate the same events with respect to their intensity* is to imagine a very different kind of history, since the subject of affective time is incommensurable with the order, and nature, of events. This was one of Lacan's best insights, and one of his advances over Freud: his insistence that the true subject of the 'impossible real' is constituted not by the subject's narrative reconstruction of his or her story but rather by the necessary *failure* of that story to include (or even to recognize) its own affective origins.[2] As Joan Copjec has written,

> Where the Foucauldian and film-theoretical positions always tend to trap the subject in representation (an idealist failing), to conceive of language as constructing the prison walls of the

subject's being, Lacan argues that the subject sees these walls as *trompe l'oeil*, and is thus constituted by something beyond them. For beyond everything that is displayed to the subject, the question is asked, 'What is being concealed from me? *What in this graphic space does not show, does not stop not writing itself?*' (1997: 34, my ital.).

The double negative in this last sentence turns what might look like passivity or absence – not writing – into an active process – *does not stop not writing*. This implies that there is something present that demands *not* to be written. Of course Lacan, and Žižek after him, would say that this 'impossible real', this 'lack' at the centre of the subject, can only be hypothesized retroactively to 'fill out' the trauma of originary absence; that the 'real' is a proleptic effect of what is always missing from representation.[3] As Copjec puts it,

> The fact that it is materially impossible to say the whole truth – that truth always backs away from language…founds the subject (1997: 35).

The truth may always back away from language, but this does not mean that we stop speaking. Sometimes, like Hamlet, the more we talk the more we back away from the truth.

To *not stop not writing* is to engage in the ceaseless production of anti-chronicle, a non-representation of what is 'really going on' in calendar time. Thus we might say that in order to comprehend any history that approaches (rather than backs away from) 'the truth', we must acknowledge that for every temporal chronicle there is an affective anti-chronicle, for every linear reconstruction of calendar events there is a constellation of significant intensities that are excluded from the story. This is not to say that affective time achieves no representation, but that we must look for it elsewhere, in the unwritten, undocumented, illegible. Any 'historicity' worthy of the name must try to 'account' not only for the linear events of calendar time but also for the non-linear 'events' of affective time, events which seek, and sometimes find, their representational truth only in the non-narrativity of bodies.

In *Hamlet*, the significant intensities of the play guarantee that an accurate calendar-history of what actually 'happened' can never be produced. Situating its protagonist within the most positivist genre in the Renaissance (the revenge tragedy), the play proceeds to dismantle all linkage between causes and effects. Hamlet's story, such as it is, takes place in the interstices of an intersubjectivity that the play always already debars. No one in this play really 'knows' or understands anyone else. Unequipped with a Habermassian life-world with which to negotiate modernity's binary divisions, Hamlet's inability to build a narrative bridge between something represented as 'objective reality' and something presented as an 'excess of affect' is precisely what keeps calling him back to the contemporary cultural stage. The problem is not that Hamlet is a 'modern' character ahead of his time, a prematurely Cartesian figure in an as yet undifferentiated social 'plenum' (Barker 1984), but that Hamlet is always already postmodern, or rather, *amodern* – since (if we follow Latour's logic) one cannot 'post' something that has not yet happened.

Hamlet occupies the awkward position of being both harbinger of, and nostalgic signifier for, the 'Modern Constitution'. Since modernity defines itself by the dual and mutually incompatible activities of 'purification' and 'mediation', its activities deny – even while fostering – the production of 'hybrids': quasi-objects or quasi-subjects which cannot properly be located on the knowledge 'map' of the moderns. What else is the ghost in *Hamlet* but just such a hybrid, a quasi-subject walking the 'unthinkable' territory between the object and subject poles? Presumably 'really there' in Act 1, its objective status is verified by 'credible and reliable' (if not well-to-do) witnesses: everyone present on the battlements sees the apparition. Later, however, when Hamlet confronts Gertrude in her chamber (3.4), the ghost's objective reality is undercut by the fact that only Hamlet sees and hears it. What exactly *is* the status of this Thing? Surely the ghost is meant, at least in Hamlet's mind, to function as a 'vanishing mediator', that element which 'although nowhere actually present... nonetheless has to be retroactively constructed, presupposed, if all other elements are to retain their consistency' (Žižek 1993: 33). But the ghost, as monstrous hybrid, will not serve its function: it 'mediates' to be sure, but refuses to 'vanish'.

Trapped in a world of conflicting epistemologies (in which the foundations of knowledge are undermined) and incommensurate ontologies (in which ghosts are released on furlough from Purgatory), Hamlet forces us to confront the fact that 'properly historicizing' is a vastly more complicated undertaking than we thought. The question we should be asking about Hamlet's dilemma is not (with all due respect to Carolyn Porter) 'are we being historical yet', but *are we being modern* yet?[4] For it is precisely in the space of a *virtual modernity* that Shakespeare pitches Hamlet's tent. Often regarded as poster boy for the nascent 'modern subject', Hamlet more closely resembles a preview of the death of the 'modern subject', if we regard that subject as a function of '"the principle of unlimited self-realization, the demand for authentic self-experience and the subjectivism of a hyperstimulated sensitivity"' (Bewes 1997: 46). As Timothy Bewes puts it, '*of course* the subject is "dead" and *has always been so* if (a) the subject and (b) "living" are conceived in idealized, modernist-derived ways' (ibid.: 46). If Latour is correct that we have never been modern, then Hamlet has never been early modern, we have never been postmodern, and we are all, along with the pesky Prince, stuck in the same boat with regard to what, exactly, 'being historicist' means.[5]

No film appropriation of Shakespeare better exemplifies the tension between narrative and apparitional histories than Gus Van Sant's 1992 film *My Own Private Idaho*. Van Sant's film takes the positivist storyline of the *Henriad* and recasts it within an explicitly postmodernized framework. Young heir Scott Favor (played by an affectless Keanu Reeves, who also plays the afore-mentioned Ted in *Bill and Ted's Excellent Adventure*) disappoints his father, Mayor Jack Favor, by being 'an effeminate boy', living a sordid street life of male prostitution. He attaches himself to a surrogate father named Bob (referred to as the 'Fat Man') who recites many of Falstaff's lines throughout the film. Ultimately renouncing Fat Bob upon his father's death, Scott claims his inheritance, marries, and returns to the bourgeois world. Despite the film's pretentiously postmodern feel and its gestures towards pastiche and *unemplotment*, it clearly advances a chronological *telos* of primogenitory advancement towards a twenty-first birthday (the age of majority), and an inheritance of the father's place in the economic and – it is hinted – the political order.

Like Hal's inheritance of the crown, Scott's inheritance is guaranteed by the passage of time. Unlike Hal, however, Scott's story is juxtaposed with another, seemingly unrelated, tableau involving Scott's beloved and narcoleptic friend Mike (also a

male hustler) and Mike's strange quest to find the elusive and
ghostly mother of his childhood. While many critics have discussed
the film's use of the *Henriad*, no one has noticed that encrypted
within the film's *Henriadic* bildungsroman is a strangely literal
and cross-gendered version of *Hamlet*. Although Scott's story
gains narrative ascendancy as the film progresses, *Private Idaho*
begins, and ends, with Mike's dilemma. Haunted by shadowy
memories of his mother and dreamlike scenes from his childhood, Mike suffers attacks of narcolepsy each time he tries to
'remember' her. His narcolepsy is an involuntary paralysis and
loss of consciousness brought on by a 'hyperstimulated sensitivity', triggered each time he tries to put his past into some kind
of narrative order – each time, in other words, he attempts to
remember 'what really happened'.

Since Scott Favor has nothing to do but 'kill time' until his
twenty-first birthday, he decides to accompany Mike on his
search for his mother. Together they represent two different
kinds of *historeme*: 'the smallest unit of historiographical fact'
(Fineman 1989: 57). For Scott, rememoration is unnecessary,
since what drives his story is the automatic, chronological telos of
patrimony. For Mike, however, the paternal metaphor has never
been present since, we discover, his biological father is actually
his older brother, Richard (a literalization of the fraternal incest
motif in *Hamlet*). Mike's historeme is matrilinear: his Big Other is
the Big Mother. Unlike Scott Favor, Mike's identity cannot be
secured by the symbolic logic of patrimonial (and patrinomial)
inheritance. Instead, his identity depends upon the epistemological return to a specifically embodied origin. In this *feminized*
version of Hamlet, the maternal historeme is the only body that
matters. In *Private Idaho*, the absence of a living mother's body
and not the presence of a dead father's spirit, becomes the film's
equally problematic vanishing mediator.

While there seems to be little resemblance between Mike's
subjective experience and Scott's, there is a crucial connection –
a Latourian 'middle' – that within the film must be disavowed in
order for the *Henriadic* element to achieve its hegemony. For
however much calendar time situates events with respect to a
series of dates, only affective time can give a sense of meaning to
history. In Scott's story, there is no mandate to carry out: there is
no love lost between father and son and the paternal signifier is

devoid both of affect and of content. For there to be any meaning or 'substance' to Scott's life, he must derive it parasitically from Mike's. Providing the affective core of Scott's *Henriad* – its 'once more into the breach' as it were – Mike's *Hamlet*, with its 'excess of affect', fills out a narrative that has been reduced to the meaningless frame of calendar time.

In *Private Idaho*, both kinds of history – calendar time and affective time – are presented. 'Put together but kept separate', purified and mediated, they lead to 'the ironic despair whose symptom is postmodernism' (Latour 1993: 67). Charting two kinds of movements – one an endless retracing of affective steps, and the other, a mere 'killing of time', the significant intensity of the former is sacrificed to the narrative logic of the latter. As the historical but empty necessity of the *Henriad* gradually takes command of the film, Mike's search for the missing Big Mother emerges as an endless search for the ghost of historical *meaning*. *Hamlet* remains, in the figure of Mike at the end of *Private Idaho*, to keep issuing the call for a history that discovers the affective truths held in, and delivered by, 'bodies that matter' (Butler 1993).

Clearly Hal and Hamlet, in whatever guise they take, have different destinies: one to ride the progression of time to a preordained inheritance and the other doomed forever to dwell in a time out of joint, paralyzed ('Heaven and earth, must I remember?' 1.2.143) by each onslaught of memory. The cynical *ennui* of the former is 'filled out' by the significant intensity of the latter. If every chronicle history depends upon the *not writing* of another story, then the vanishing mediator does not really 'vanish' after all; instead, it retreats to the 'space between two deaths'. As Žižek suggests, this is also a place

> of sublime beauty as well as terrifying monsters,... the site of das Ding, of the real-traumatic kernel in the midst of symbolic order. This place opened up by symbolization/historicization: the process of historicization implies an empty place, a non-historical kernel around which the symbolic network is articulated (1989: 135).

Although the 'place between two deaths' is opened up by symbolization/historicization, that place is never originally empty. As an object to be remembered achieves critical *affective* mass, it threatens to produce a catastrophic sleep and a forgetting. Once affective experience reaches a certain pitch, production of an 'accurate' narrative history becomes difficult indeed.

This is the real ghost of *Hamlet*. Not the ghost of a murdered king but the spectre of a play that serves as an anti-chronicle to the *Henriad*, its proleptic condition of possibility, its challenge, from the world of apparitions to the *Henriad*'s positivist historiography. In *Private Idaho*'s *Henriad manque*, we see an elegy for a patriarchal legacy that has been emptied of meaning and affect. In its place, we see a turn to maternal origin as a substitute for a Big Other that can no longer issue a believable mandate. *Private Idaho* demonstrates that without the 'che vuoi?', without the belief that something more is required of the subject than impassively riding the passage of time, there can only be subjective destitution – an historical narcolepsy that returns the 'unclaimed' subject, again and again, to the same road leading nowhere.

Which is precisely where Mike ends up. The film closes not with Scott Favor's ascension to the place of the father, but with Mike's return to the same barren highway on which he began. The film's opening frame offers a definition of the word narcolepsy. Its closing frame says 'Have a nice day.' We begin with unconsciousness and end with a command to *enjoy our time*. But it is not historical time we are instructed to enjoy. In this evacuated equivalent of the paternal injunction we hear the mantra delivered robotically by salesclerks and bank tellers, whose event horizons are determined by the daily rhythms of their employers, corporations, and the Dow Jones – a world in which (like Scott Favor's) time is simply money and nothing more. 'Have a nice day' (on your road leading nowhere) is the motto of virtual history. Its lack of both symbolic and libidinal investment heralds the cynicism that makes it nearly impossible to have a meaningful conversation with the living. This is the real crisis of historicity.

The representation of calendar time carries a legacy composed of the 'indivisible remainder' that ghosts it. Every son who picks up the father's sceptre has a mortified double who wanders, forever asking the question, 'Now, mother, what's the matter?' (*Hamlet* 3.4.9). To say this is not to claim that women are the site of affective meaning, but to point out that in the kind of historiography that underwrites patriarchal culture, *whatever* is the 'not written' will constitute the Hamlet-effect. Every *Henriad* produces a *Hamlet* as its symptom.

The larger object in question, to return to the road on which we began, is the figure of Shakespeare himself, who currently signifies 'the historical' for us. Contemporary fetishizing of Shakespeare enjoins an historical narcolepsy not unlike Mike's: one in which we attempt to locate ourselves as historical subjects by turning and returning to a 'corpus' that we believe embodies the truth of our history for us. Like the Big Mother, Shakespeare offers the fantasy of a 'common' origin in which we might all find ourselves represented. That we continue to demonstrate a cultural need for a body of *significant* intensity (as opposed to the empty intensities with which we are constantly bombarded by mass media) does not signal theoretical naiveté, nor nostalgia for a mythical 'centred subject'. It does suggest, however, that something has gone missing in historicists' way of dividing up time, something is being left out by its divisions of 'eras only in terms of successive revolutions' (Latour 1993: 46). The complexities and experiences of affective time will always proliferate in ways not mappable on a radar only designed to look for 'successive revolutions'. To this extent, the very idea that there can be such a 'thing' as an 'historicized subject' of early, mid-, or post-modernity is a critical fiction. Hamlet continues to speak to us because he continues to be 'timeless': not because he 'transcends' history but because *we were never early modern.*

The Hamlet Formerly Known as Prince

The Whine of '99: Everyone's getting rich but me!
     – cover legend, *Newsweek*, July 5, 1999

The last few years of the millennium saw a *Hamlet* boom unmatched since the onset of American mass media. The prince who in Shakespeare's play literally ends up nowhere (dying in a state that is neither quite Denmark nor Norway) now walks everywhere among us, a ghost in mass culture, from 'light' comedies or adventure movies like *LA Story* and *Last Action Hero* to venues as ambitious as Branagh's bombastic 1996 film version and Almereyda's post-Wall Street film version.[1] The play has always been a rich repository of Shakespearean sound bites and clichés. But this alone does not tell us much about why *Hamlet* in particular has enjoyed such a startling re-emergence into popular prominence. The same figure whose failure to inherit and refusal to take the throne in Denmark leads to the death of his state has somehow become (perhaps on the basis of this refusal) the 'unofficial legislator' of the millennial 'democratic man' – the man who would, and would not, be King.

But what can middle-class Americans possibly have in common with this Prince? The dictum (by now long familiar in high school classrooms) that Hamlet is the Everyman of the human condition, caught between desire and duty, conscience and cowardice, religion and revenge, passion and reason, has grown hoarfrost. If we look at Hamlet's actual political status in the play, no one could be less an Everyman: first, Hamlet – as sole heir of a royal father – is a prince; second, he is at the centre of all the other characters' attentions. Everyone in this play is obsessed with taking Hamlet's pulse; and in this regard at the very least, he is even more king than the king.

Despite all this, Hamlet 'insists on removing himself from events that he is nevertheless at the center of'.[2] Thus we might say that Hamlet's simultaneous lack of political interest and self-righteous aggrievement have created a cultural 'wormhole', whisking him out of Shakespeare's era and dropping him squarely into our own. Middle-class Americans can be said to share Hamlet's general dissatisfaction, nervous boredom, and self-righteousness. We have, however, something that Hamlet seems to lack – an aggressive sense of entitlement to ever more of whatever is available. Why is it that we who are not 'heirs apparent' keep demanding more royalties and privileges while Hamlet – a prince – evinces no desire for what he is literally entitled to? In a play in which everyone else knows exactly what they want (except Ophelia, whose desires are sacrificed to the agendas of father, brother, and king), whether it is sex, status, money, land, or authority, Hamlet will have none of it, and becomes during the course of the play a 'nation' unto himself. In the cultural milieu of late Elizabethan England, in a play which is resolutely patriarchal, monarchical, and nationalistic, this is (to say the least) an untenable position for Hamlet to take. Veering between grandiosity and abjection, Hamlet will neither suffer to be governed nor assume the responsibility of governing others.

Patriarchy, monarchy, and empire: these are the ideological and political foundations of Shakespeare's England. They are also the dominant (although by no means only) arbitrageurs of desire, designating what men of standing are expected to want and thereby imposing what is supposed to be, ideologically at least, a shared basis for masculine identity. In theory, however, this troika is no longer the basis of American culture. After all, America is not a monarchy but a democracy; Hamlet cannot be 'us'. Most Americans do not stand to inherit entire nations from their fathers (even if they are their namesakes) and their 'entitlements' are considerably more vague than those Hamlet can and should lay claim to. And yet throughout the course of the play, Hamlet will claim nothing except to 'have that within which passes show' (1.2.85).[3]

This invisible 'that' to which Hamlet refers has been the source of considerable confusion and speculation, in critical analyses of the play as well as in mass cultural film versions. Most literate Americans realize when they hear the name 'Hamlet' that something important is being invoked, and yet no one (including Shakespeare scholars such as myself) knows exactly what that might be. If nothing else, we know that Hamlet stands for Big Ideas, especially ideas that rebel against corruption of some kind. Mention Hamlet to the average middle-class American and certain things spring to mind: romance, high culture, adolescence, high school English, failed exams, revenge, procrastination, and other vague themes related and unrelated. What does not seem to register with most people is an awareness that Hamlet is a prince who should, by the time the play begins, be a king.[4]

When the pop musician Prince Rogers Nelson decided to abandon his stage name Prince (replacing it with an unpronounceable glyph), he stated to the world that the title by which we knew him no longer denoted him truly. While this gesture resulted only in a more annoying name (the Artist-Formerly-Known-as-Prince) it is not the first time a Prince has disavowed his title. Like 'the Artist' (who has since, sensibly, returned to his name), Prince Hamlet can neither inhabit nor escape a title that trails him like an embarrassing odor. Along with Prince Hal of the *Henriad*, Hamlet bears two paternal signifiers – royal and patrinomial. But while Hal may be called many things during his sojourn in Eastcheap, he is never NOT a 'Prince', never not understood to be a future king. Here then are the two most paradigmatic sons in the Shakespearean corpus – Hal, who cannot choose not be a king and Hamlet, who cannot choose to be one. Both are set up to repay debts they 'never promised' (*I Henry IV*, 1.3.187); both struggle with the after-effects of paternal errors in judgement; both turn to clownish surrogate fathers (Falstaff and Yorick, respectively); and both face 'doubles' who show them how they should be doing their jobs (Hotspur and Fortinbras). Hal and Hamlet represent a dilemma that clearly obsessed Shakespeare: What exactly is the nature and function of a 'proper' patrimony? What are the requirements of leaving a legacy? What are fathers supposed to pass down to their sons and what are sons expected to give in return? And what happens when entitlement – political, legal, or affective – ceases to be a motivating factor for individual agency?[5]

Patrimony consists of two structures, the first nominal or patronymic, and the second (equally laden with symbolism) biological. A father must designate his heir and dispose of his monies accordingly in his last will and testament. There are, after all, 'testes' in the etymology of 'testimony': they share the same Latin root, *testis* – which means to bear witness. They also share the root *testa*, which means both the 'skin or coating of a seed', and 'that by which the existence, quality, or genuineness of anything is, or may be determined', a 'means of trial'. To testiculate is to encase or join together elements within a sac or enclosure; to testificate is to certify a fact in documented form.[6] It is no mere metaphor that a testament is a document wherein a father's will and his goods conjoin, forming a legal 'coating' (figuratively speaking) over his seed. This is the same conflation of meaning crudely familiar in references to 'the family jewels', and so on. But the implications of this hybrid legal term, in which the morphology of a male body part is allegorized in juridical form, demonstrate that in Shakespeare's culture (as in our own), there is no biology that is not also politically symbolic.

That this was understood in early modern England was clear in the passage of 'perpetual entail' laws in 1557, which designated that even fathers themselves are subordinated to the rules of patrimony. Just as a royal son is expected, barring dementia or incapacity, to succeed his father, so too must a father properly transmit his 'testament' to his son. In this way, patrimony functions as a *prosthesis*: a legal structure grafted onto a living body, technically and ideologically inalienable from that body. In early modern culture, time must be understood *biosymbolically* as the matriculation of the social relationship from the body of the father to that of his issue. Organized by patrilinear successive monarchy, the passage of political time is inseparable from biological time: the father's body is the political calendar. To say this is not to naturalize the way in which patriarchy works, but to point out that in such a culture, the legal disposition of the father's place, position, property, and name is expected to flow in the same direction as his semen. The 'money shot' is not a concept invented by the pornography industry; patrimony in its original conception is the linkage between testes and testament.[7]

Throughout Shakespeare's plays there are many offspring whose stances towards their fathers can best be phrased as 'show me the money'.[8] In the tragedies, as well as in many of the comedies, conflicts are usually engendered by paternal (and/or royal) failure to properly testificate or testiculate. Shakespeare's concern with the deformations of paternal and political legacies also runs through both history tetralogies. Despite, however, all its acute tensions between fathers and sons, the *Henriad* represents a triumphant recuperation of patrimonial logic under the conditions of extreme ideological and economic restructuring underway in Elizabethan England. From *Richard II*, in which the 'sublime object' of royal ideology is presumably – and mistakenly – embodied solely in the Monarch, to *Henry V*, in which every Englishman becomes a shareholder in the sublime corporation of England as represented by King Harry's crown, the law of patrimonial reproduction survives its symbolic transformations. The redistribution of sublime Matter, which takes all four plays of the second tetralogy to accomplish, ensures (temporarily at least) that anyone who attacks the monarchy attacks as well the body of the corporate shareholders, for whom the monarch is now less the embodiment than the guarantor.

Patrimony in the *Henriad* is rendered functional again by Hal's construction of a hybrid paternity that grafts his father's body human onto Richard's body sublime – masterfully creating a legacy that can be legitimated precisely by being disconnected *to any one particular father*. Hal's homage to the usurped 'sun king' (his royal reburial of Richard II and paid mourners' rites) renders him the symbolic offspring of Richard II (and therefore entitled to inherit symbolic legitimacy from Richard), even while the play makes it clear that he is Henry's biological son. In this way, 'King Harry' manages to protect and even promote patrimonial legitimacy by decentralizing its location, making every Tom, Dick, or Francis a 'brother' to himself and thereby a symbolic 'son' to Henry IV.

Of course this recuperation is not without fissures. As Lisa Jardine has written about the *Henriad*, 'there is a straight contradiction between lineage and conquest', and 'in the formation of national identity there is an inevitable tension between royal marriage (in which two partners come from different nations, and may effect a cross-national territorial merger) and the passing on of the crown by lineal descent' (1996: 10). The tenuous nature of the legal claims Henry V makes on France are 'fudged', as Jardine puts it, by his 'successful' courtship of the French princess Catherine. Thus the *Henriad* secures patrimony at the expense of 'a doubt about the general possibility of effecting such lineal transactions without the weakening intercession of women' (1996: 10). Patrimonial entail may be protected by marriage, but patrilineal purity is inevitably diluted by sexual reproduction.

In *Hamlet,* a particular father is very much the issue; and phobia about the corrupting 'seepage' of women into the pure 'stock' of the father is everywhere apparent. If patrimony requires the begetting of heirs, Hamlet will not comply. For Hamlet, all children are women's children and therefore tainted by corruption. As Janet Adelman has argued (1992), 'the structure of Hamlet...is marked by the struggle...to free the masculine identity of both father and son from its origin in the contaminated maternal body' (1992: 7–24 *passim*). This struggle – so evident in *Hamlet* and indeed as Adelman's work has shown, in many of Shakespeare's plays – also defines one of the key goals of the 'testamentary' process more generally. Patrimony, properly understood, is designed to suppress maternal origin and substitute the paternal 'will' as the site of plenitude for both cultural and material capital. However, Hamlet's refusal of reproduction is more than just a misogynist repudiation of women, since women are for Hamlet the 'identified' symptom of much more threatening realization. Encrypted within Hamlet's refusal to reproduce is an awareness that he is always already the reproduced, that his fate is to serve as 'back-up' to a father who refuses, in Marjorie Garber's memorable phrase, to 'give up the ghost' (Garber 1987: 124).

King Hamlet continues to govern from beyond the grave and seems oblivious to Hamlet's political rights as royal heir. There have of course been long-standing critical debates about whether or not Hamlet's Denmark is an elective monarchy, since the status of the actual Danish Constitution (as implemented by the group of aristocratic landowners known as the Rigsråd) included a proviso for a monarch to be elected (Hibbard 1987: 37). Whether or not Shakespeare would have known about the Danish Constitution is to some extent moot; even if he had, Danish history shows that by 1448 the Oldenberg dynasty began with Christian I (Sohmer 1996: 21) and, apart from civil skirmishes provoked by Catholic bishops and nobles out of fear of encroaching Lutheranism, the throne remained in the hands of Oldenberg heirs. In 1536 Christian III took the throne, which then went to his son Frederick in 1559. In 1588 Frederick's son Christian IV succeeded and reigned until 1648 (ibid.). In other words, during Shakespeare's entire lifetime Denmark was a *de facto* successive monarchy, since the Rigsråd always 'elected' the King's oldest son. Consequently it is not necessarily contradictory that Shakespeare would mention election in a play that so clearly stacks the deck for succession – a play entitled *The Tragedy of Hamlet: Prince of Denmark*.

It is, however, strange – since references to election are few and fleeting in the play, notably at 5.2, when Hamlet refers to Claudius as he that 'Popped in between the election and my hopes' (5.2.66); and at the end of the scene when Hamlet, in his dying moments, prophesies that 'the election lights/On Fortinbras' (5.2.297–8). In both instances these references are conspicuously jarring. First, everyone in the play behaves as if Hamlet's right to succeed his father were a given; presumably, therefore, he does not need election as anything other than perhaps a formality. Second, Fortinbras hardly needs the election either, since his army has occupied Denmark by main force. Perhaps Shakespeare knew that although Denmark had an electoral provision in its Constitution, it was no longer operative. If this is the case, raising the question of election in the play serves only to further emphasize the shadiness of the legacy King Hamlet has bequeathed to the prince.

Thus the play begins with a strange paradox: everyone talks as if the throne were Hamlet's birthright, yet *no one* questions why Claudius occupies it. This political double-consciousness weaves the mechanisms of deferral, displacement, and delay into the operations of the state itself. But what exactly is Hamlet's patrimony? What has the dead King actually willed to his only son? As Richard Wilson informs us, by the middle of the sixteenth century, ' "an older grid of inheritance," with its lateral network of social affiliations and obligations, was abandoned for a new documentary and legal system of transmission, focused on selected lineal descendants' (1993: 187). Even if an 'afflicted testator' wished to disinherit his immediate lineal successors, freedom of testation

was circumscribed by the tradition that when a man died
leaving wife and issue, only one-third of his estate was devisable
by will, while a third went to his wife as dower and the other to
his children. Entitlement of heirs was further safeguarded by
canons of descent which ruled that inheritance was patrilinear,
an heir could never be disinherited (1993: 188).

Certainly an heir could not be disinherited if the first born, or
sole issue, were a son.

Despite the clarity of expectation entail was designed to
guarantee, nowhere in *Hamlet* is there any explicit mention of
the dead King's will.[9] However, while a king might literally die
intestate, a king cannot effectually die intestate, for the entire
royal structure is built on direct linear succession of property,
authority, and monies. Even if we were to speculate about the
divisions of King Hamlet's personal estate upon his death in
terms of the necessary third being allotted to wife and issue, it is
hardly likely that the Old king would have used his freedom of
testation to bequeath the remaining third to Claudius. If as the
ghost rails, Claudius 'won to his shameful lust / the will of my
most seeming-virtuous queen', that would still leave him with
only a third of a claim to the kingdom (Gertrude's 'will' or
portion) – with Hamlet being by default the two-thirds shareholder, more than enough upon which to base a claim to the
throne. As Eric Mallin has argued, 'as much as [Hamlet]
denies his stature, however, it remains obvious to the other
characters' (1996: 111), and especially to Laertes, who warns
Ophelia not to set her sights above her station since Hamlet 'is
subject to his birth' (1.3.18). But if his 'will is not his own', as
Laertes puts it, it is not because 'his choice must be
circumscribed / Unto the voice and yielding of that body /
Whereof he is the head'. It is because his father has not left a
will; and despite Hamlet's obvious legal right to do so, he will
not step forward to claim any inheritance that has not been
articulated by his father.

What is most surprising about Hamlet's 'unassuming' stance is
how unsurprising it becomes as the play progresses. Despite the
overdetermination of being a paternal namesake, there is an
almost complete lack of identification between Hamlet and his
father. In his first soliloquy, he compares Claudius to the King

and finds him 'no more like my father / Than I to Hercules' (1.2.152–3), a comparison which suggests that Claudius's lack of resemblance to his father can be measured in terms of his own. Thus Hamlet seems to have identity without identification, situating himself outside of the reflective filiations of politics, friendship (with the exception of Horatio), and love. He retains only the name and none of the 'addition of a king'. As Mallin nicely puts it, 'something weird has happened to the procedure, not just the outcome, of the succession' (1996: 112).

When Laertes refers to the 'body' of which Hamlet 'is the head', he speaks of Denmark, the King's sublime body, and by extension, his subjects. But the body of Denmark seems to have undergone a strange entropy, its exact boundaries becoming amorphous and semipermeable. There is already a *de facto* divorce between the 'body' and 'head' of state; and it was first effected not by Claudius but *by King Hamlet himself*, before the play even begins. When Marcellus asks his fellow sentinals

> Why this same strict and most observant watch
> So nightly toils the subject of the land
> And why such daily cast of brazen cannon
> And foreign mart for implements of war (1.1.74–7).

Horatio answers that King Hamlet, long ago 'pricked on by a most emulate pride' (1.1.86) staked a major portion of his kingdom on a wager with King Fortinbras of Norway. Both fathers were prepared capriciously to gamble away their sons' patrimonies in a duel, thereby breaking the laws of entail that in Shakespeare's day bound fathers as well as sons. That King Hamlet won the wager would lead, one might think, to this story being trumpeted to general acclaim. Instead, Horatio tells Bernardo how 'the whisper goes', suggesting something shameful in the enterprise. After all, the outcome of the bet might have gone the other way. King Hamlet may not have broken the letter of entail, but he broke its spirit, treating his kingdom as if it were his private property and acting as if he had (or would have) no sons to whom he might one day have to answer. While one hesitates to speculate about young Hamlet's 'childhood', his father's cavalier disregard for his offspring's political future seems to have registered in the prince. When Hamlet tells Horatio that he does not hold his life at a pin's fee he reveals that although he has a title, he does not have what a title is meant to convey: a sense of entitlement.

For Hamlet to take the throne upon his father's death would be to proclaim himself heir and go after what is rightfully his, despite his father's 'will', or lack thereof. After all, young Fortinbras is doing so, 'sharking up a list of landlesse resolutes' and aiming to 'recover of us by strong hand / And terms compulsatory those foresaid lands / So by his father lost' (1.1.104–6). Frequently noticed is the fact that Fortinbras is in a political situation analogous to Hamlet's: his uncle Norway now sits on his father's throne. But Fortinbras refuses to accept 'the same cov'nant / and carriage of the article design'd '(95–6) by his father and King Hamlet. The elliptical way in which the 'seal'd compact' was struck (as described by Horatio, who provides the only narrative we get about the event) suggests that Denmark and Norway were not technically at war prior to the carriage of the article designed but rather that the conditions of war were originally 'prick'd on' by the compulsive masculine competition between the two kings.

When the ghost describes the details of his murder and Claudius's guilt, what he *should* do is urge Hamlet to proclaim himself the lawful heir of Denmark, reclaim his throne from a foul usurper, and prosecute him for fratricide, regicide, usurpation, and unlawful marriage. But this would not be in keeping with what Horatio describes as the ghost's 'extravagant and erring spirit' (1.1.159). After all, such a revenge would be *legal*, and would take into account his son's interests as well as protect the future of Denmark. But what has Hamlet's father to do with laws, either of nature or of culture? Therefore, the ghost's only 'will' is to revenge and remember him. A legal proceeding against Claudius would take into account the crime committed against the son as well as against the father, for in patrimonial culture there is no crime against the latter that does not affect the former. Irrespective of where one stands on the issue of elective monarchy in Denmark, for an Elizabethan audience, as Lisa Jardine points out, 'Claudius's marriage to Gertrude historically...is...unlawful...and...it deprives Hamlet of his lawful succession' (1996: 39). Given that Hamlet clearly registers the 'offense' done to his father that, according to Ecclesiastical law, makes the marriage unlawful, he could legitimately step forward, declare the marriage invalid and Claudius a usurper. Especially since, according to Jardine, 'the offence is against Hamlet; the offending party is Claudius' (1996: 45).

The procedure of patriarchal succession must be based on the unquestioned blood linkage between father and son. We are never given to know how long Claudius skulked about the court at Elsinore or what his role was prior to the King's murder. Nowhere is there a fully convincing explanation of why Gertrude agrees to her admittedly 'oer-hasty marriage' (2.2.57) and why 'no one utters a peep of protest about Claudius's ascent' (Mallin 1996: 113). Unless we accept Hamlet's view of Gertrude's nymphomania (which I do not, since we never see Gertrude acting even remotely lascivious), his failure to challenge the succession – coupled with Gertrude's inexplicable willingness to see her son bypassed – raises the possibility that Claudius could be Hamlet's biological father (something more than hinted at in Branagh's 1996 film, in which Branagh's Hamlet was made closely to resemble Derek Jacobi's Claudius). At the very least, this would go a long way towards explaining why the dead king left no provision for Hamlet, and does not insist that he claim the throne.

One need not argue, however, that Claudius must be Hamlet's 'real' father, only that Hamlet's paternity is a question raised in many ways throughout the play.[10] Veiled disavowals of paternity are detectable in the way the ghost never addresses Hamlet directly as 'son' but rather resorts to a grammar of indirection, calling Hamlet 'thou noble youth'. His references to himself as 'thy father's spirit' are usually couched in syllogism: 'if thou has nature in thee' (1.5.81), and 'if thou didst ever thy dear father love' (1.5.23). It is less interesting, however, to try to make a case for Claudius's paternity than it is to notice that the space created by the doubt is filled with a series of *paternity tests*, in which both the nature and culture of the ties between fathers and sons are strained to the limits of credibility.

Even if the play showcases Fortinbras as an exemplar of the son's right and expectation directly to succeed his father, can we hold him up as the model son? While he is preparing to reclaim his birthright, he is also *explicitly going against his father's will*. His actions clearly show that 'all bets are off' between dead fathers, and that a 'compact' between fathers cannot be honoured at the expense of the covenant that binds fathers and sons. Fortinbras makes no claims beyond the recovery of those lands that were by his father lost, demonstrating that he well understands both the spirit and the letter of perpetual entail. To this extent Fortinbras is a 'model' of the path Hamlet might take. But if everyone in the play turns a blind eye to the explicitly political nature of Claudius's crime, it is because Hamlet himself does so. He seems to know in his bones that the ghost's real mandate is, *remember me, revenge me, but do not replace me.*

A dilemma, since to be a prince is to be a future king. If the possibility for the latter is annulled, the former is emptied of substance – an only son and first-born royal heir cannot be a once and future prince. The designations King and Prince only have meaning in the relation of linear succession; without such a framework, the only part of the father's title that carries forward to the son is the patronym 'Hamlet'. In this scenario, the political inheritance that should derive from biological reproduction has been replaced by the mere repetition of the patronym; and the very concept of 'patrimony' is suborned, since reproducing the name, without 'the addition of a king', takes the testes out of the testament.

The manifest narcissism King Hamlet demonstrated in his days of nature is more than matched by the pathological self-obsession of his days in Purgatory. He does not seem to care who is on the throne as long as it is not Claudius. The conceptual fantasy being played out beneath the ghost's disregard of Hamlet's patrimony has a contemporary analogue, and I think it can profitably illustrate the political psychology that drives the play. That analogue is something we call cloning. As Jean Baudrillard has argued, cloning is

> The dream, then, of an eternal twinning as replacement for sexual procreation, with its link to death. A cellular dream of scissiparity – the purest form of parenthood in that it allows us at last to dispense with the other and go directly from one to the same (1993: 114).

Obviously, Shakespeare's culture could not imagine a technology in which cloning would be possible. But Shakespeare could certainly conceptualize cloning as a fantasmatic *allegorical form*, one which leaves its imprint every time a son is named for his father. When the ghost commands Hamlet to 'remember me', the effect is not ideological 'interpellation' but rather scissipation – the process of being cut, divided, or split. The ghost's command-ment reveals a profoundly disturbing fantasy at the heart of patrimonial culture, one that can even be seen in Shakespeare's final revisions to his own 'last will and testament': a fantasy of keeping one's 'essence' pure, free of the contamination of Other-ness; a dream of exercising in perpetuity one's undivided will by eradicating the difference that inevitably attends succession. Succession is by nature supercession; in order to hand something down one must let it go. This is what the ghost of old Hamlet cannot bring himself to do.

To be a first-born son under primogeniture is one thing; to bear the father's name is a doubly derivative legacy that leaves little room for any kind of autonomy. The result in *Hamlet* is not a myth of self-genesis, since as Baudrillard argues,

> such phantasies always involve the figures of the mother and the father – sexed parental figures whom the subject may indeed yearn to eliminate, the better to usurp their positions, but this in no sense implies contesting the symbolic structure of procreation: if you become your own child, you are still the child of someone. Cloning, on the other hand, radically eliminates not only the mother, but also the father, for it eliminates the interaction between his genes and the mother's, the imbrication of the parents' difference, and above all, *the joint act of procreation* (1993: 114–15, italics mine).

Bound by his father to enact his will without succeeding him, Hamlet becomes a scissoid replicant – a creature meant to go perpetually from the one to the same. 'Remember me' means just that – remember only me, while the maternal body is effaced from the relation. The king's sublime body – here manifest in his commandment – cannot 'Live / within the book and volume of [Hamlet's] brain / unmixed with baser matter', unless the son agrees to be the father's clone.

What would the stakes of such an agreement be? No less than the dissolution of the subject, since 'identical duplication ends the division that constitutes him' (Baudrillard 1993: 115). As Baudrillard evocatively puts it, cloning eradicates the mirror stage,

the timeless narcissistic dream of the subject's projection into
an ideal alter ego – for the projection too works by means of an
image – the image in the mirror, in which the subject becomes
alienated in order to rediscover himself...Nothing of all this is
left with cloning. No more mediations – no more images: an
individual product on a conveyer belt is in no sense a reflection
of the next (albeit identical) product in line. The one is never a
mirage, whether ideal or mortal, of the other: they can only
accumulate (1993: 115).

Is this not in effect what the ghost is asking of his son? That he
act without either reflection or differentiation? The distinction
that should constitute Hamlet as a subject is precisely the one his
father will not recognize. And since successive monarchy (and to
some extent all patrimony) depends upon a patriarchal fantasy of
cloning – that sons will be the 'True Originall Copies' of their
fathers – Hamlet's implied lack of resemblance to his father visu-
ally raises the spectre of adultery, thereby forcing Gertrude and
the joint act of procreation back into the picture, a sure-fire way
to counteract the maternal erasure at the centre of patriarchal
will power.[11]

In *Hamlet*, the time is out of joint because the elaborate political and social mechanism of filiation is broken even while it is
obsessively insisted upon at the level of the signifier. This is the
remarkable fact of 'plot' that Claudius, perhaps the most
successful straw man in literary history, obscures: that the throne
of Denmark was imperiled initially by King Hamlet himself; that
Hamlet's displacement from the throne was first 'practised',
however fantasmatically, by his own father; that the first crime
we hear about in the play was the enactment, through the wager
with Fortinbras, of a symbolic filicide. The way the play invokes,
and then induces us to forget, how the whisper went occludes the
failure of entailment on both ends: the fathers' refusal to will
entailed property to sons and the son's refusal to provide heirs.
Rife with unclaimed patrimonies, *Hamlet* stages the ways in
which the patrimonial ideal of eternal twinning is incommensurable with the fact of flesh and blood heirs. Thus it reveals a
parody of differentiation at the heart of patriarchal culture and
the subsequent fragility of a political inheritance rooted in
primogeniture.

In its representation of a bankrupt paternal legacy, Hamlet's Denmark is closer in many ways to the spirit of contemporary America than it is to Shakespearean England. For all that has been written about Hamlet as forerunner of the modern subject, his 'fate' more closely resembles that of the Replicants in Ridley Scott's 1989 film *Blade Runner*: to be driven by 'memories' of a familial relationship that the play suggests never existed. Scott's Replicants (cyborgs who are human in every way but biological origin) are haunted by a vague sense that their memories of childhood and family life are as fabricated as they are, even as they cling to these memories as evidence that they exist as real human beings. The most heartbreaking moments in the film occur when these creatures discover that their memories are not their own but rather have been downloaded into their mental technology by their scientist creator. Even a presumably post-modernist – if not posthumanist – fiction such as *Blade Runner* harbours a humanistic yearning insofar as it underscores the necessity of narrative memory in the creation of subjectivity. Even Replicants need to be able to tell stories about themselves.

Hamlet's pledge of allegiance to the ghost's commandment paradoxically constitutes the very memories he can now claim to have sacrificed for his father:

> Remember thee?
> Ay, thou poor ghost, while memory holds a seat
> In this distracted globe. Remember thee?
> Yea, from the table of my memory
> I'll wipe away all trivial fond records,
> All saws of books, all forms, all pressures past,
> That youth and observation copied there,
> And thy commandment all alone shall live
> Within the book and volume of my brain
> Unmixed with baser matter (1.5.95–104).

In the gesture of renouncing his own 'history' (whatever that may have been) Hamlet retroactively ratifies 'all pressures past', 'all trivial fond records'; in their place he downloads his father's history, his father's heavily edited 'memories', his father's sexual jealousy of Gertrude and Claudius. Like the Replicants, however, just because Hamlet's memories are not his own does not mean he is not nostalgic. Hamlet may look and act nothing like his father, but he can at least attempt to model the *prosthetic subjectivity* that his father expects of his dream clone.

After all, one does not need a new story to produce a clone: the only history that matters is the donor's. The real promised end of cloning is that it enables reproduction without the messy and unpredictable interference of other narratives. By neither generating nor requiring new bio-allegiances or kinship networks, cloning makes the passage of political time irrelevant, if not redundant. Unlike cloning, sexual reproduction always generates a new story – the participation of women, the creation of new bloodlines and genetic configurations, new filiations, and the potential, inevitably, for a changing politics. Patriarchal primogeniture and the fantasy of narcissistic protectionism it offers to powerful fathers is the 'early modern' conceptual equivalent of cloning, and it runs throughout Shakespeare's corpus, long before twentieth-century medical technology was able to say Hello Dolly.

Perhaps this is why plot is so famously hamstrung in *Hamlet*. Time *is* out of joint – and in an alarmingly literal way. The play ferrets out the refusal, deeply encoded in the heart of patrimonial legacy, to permit sons (or daughters) to supercede – or even abandon altogether – their fathers' wills of what the future should be. This kind of 'timelessness' resists new narratives and disallows the revolutions of history that inevitably occur when one generation ushers in the next. Shakespeare's *Hamlet* 'stands the test of time', insofar as in the arrested development of its fathers we can see a vision of the future: the ability to worship at the shrine of self offered by our own DNA – the choice, now technologically foreseeable, to become our own offspring. Had this prospect been available to Hamlet's father I have little doubt that he would have availed himself of it.

In *Hamlet*, Shakespeare reveals the structural narcissism at the heart of primogeniture and by extension linear royal descent. In doing so, he suggests – deliberately or not – that the process of inheriting a throne or position of power is *fundamentally anti-political*. A politics by definition negotiates contestatory claims and positions rather than a static situation in which all power relations are 'givens'. It is no accident, therefore, that in *Hamlet*, adultery – and not the ghost – becomes the biggest spectre. Adultery brings exogenous sexual politics into a marriage, thereby threatening the static biological arrangements that marriage is supposed to guarantee and the property relations based on bloodline that it is meant to secure. The most frightening thing perhaps about the spectre of adultery in *Hamlet*, and in early modern culture more generally, may be the way in which its threat of dubious paternity holds the mirror of biological nature up against the fantasy of juridical cloning effected by primogeniture and the legal subsumption of women's identities to those of fathers and husbands.

Their fixation on Gertrude's sexuality ultimately obscures for Hamlet *pere et fils* a political situation of far greater import: the survival of Denmark itself. *Hamlet* is a play about a nation sidetracked to death by the 'rank sweat of an enseaméd bed' (3.4.85). This alone makes it the poster play for American politics with its (penultimate) political scandal at the end of the millennium: the impeachment of President William Jefferson Clinton. Independent Counsel Kenneth Starr began with the task of investigating one possible crime – the Whitewater real estate swindle – only to lead us into a quagmire of sexual and familial betrayal. As Laura Kipnis has put it, 'even if *Time* [Magazine] hadn't designated Bill Clinton "Libido in Chief"', you'd have to have been in a coma this decade not to notice that politician adultery is occupying an inordinate amount of the nation's attention' (1998: 314). In this case *Time* is not out of joint: rather, it exemplifies the extent to which Americans have ceased to function as political citizens and instead become – like Hamlet, whether they want to or not – a nation of sexual detective/revengers.

Our obsession with sexual fidelity as a 'protective talisman' (Kipnis 1998: 315) of political character and stability differs little from Hamlet's. The main difference is in the nature of our idealism about the 'Fathers' of our Nation. Americans do not subscribe (not consciously at least) to the Medieval political theology of the King's Two Bodies. We do not believe that our highest officials – whether Supreme Court Justices or Presidents – partake of this second, 'divine' body that makes the flesh of those people more exalted than our own. Nevertheless, we continue to act as if we do, replicating the Hamlet scenario and continuing to insist that our leaders be Hyperions to our Satyrs.

But no matter how many crimes our social detectives uncover about our best and brightest, the cynicism they leave in

their wake is more than compensated for by the thrill, the
frisson, of discovering that Americans are still closet idealists;
that we are capable of feeling something – anything – intensely
about our leaders and therefore about ourselves. We feel most
betrayed not by any particular act our leaders may have
committed, but by the way they puncture our dual American
(and Hamletian!) fetishes of Transcendence and Innocence. It
would be a mistake, however, to dismiss all this as an example
of American 'Puritanism', or the hypocrisy of a culture that
wallows in prurience. Americans speculate about politicians'
sex lives not because we really want to find them 'guilty' but
because as long as we are suspicious, as psychoanalyst Adam
Phillips has put it, 'it makes us believe that there is something
to know, and something that is worth knowing' (Kipnis 1998: 316).
In Phillips' view,

> Adultery is...at heart a drama about change. It's a way of
> trying to invent a world, and a way of knowing something
> about what we may want: by definition, then, a political form
> (ibid.: 314).

As we have seen, in *Hamlet* adultery is the only political form;
political stability, succession, and even national survival all
dissolve in the wake of King Hamlet's voracious sexual narcissism
and the deformed legacy it bequeaths the prince.

Shakespeare's fascination with the violent coercion of identity
exacted by paternal legacy vexes his entire corpus, which is full
of children who cannot, or will not, be 'like' their fathers (or their
mothers, for that matter). For all the devastation this tension
generates, Shakespeare shows us time and again that the only
route to political change is through *the lack of resemblance* between
parents and offspring.[12] *Hamlet* offers no recuperable models
of paternal sublimity, nothing with which to reconstitute the
foundation of the royal state. In his refusal to take up the crown,
a wife, the state, and father offspring, Hamlet breaks the
continuity of production that would enable the dream of patriarchal 'inevitability' to continue. He can only, with his dying
voice, give Denmark away to Fortinbras, the most perfect clone
in the Shakespearean corpus.

Hamlet is a play for contemporary America, with its deep
uncertainty about what kinds of stories to tell about its public

figures (and by extension, ourselves) and what kind of government Americans wish to subscribe to. Is America an elective or a successive democracy? What difference does or should it make if a presidential successor is a namesake? In spite of itself, and in keeping with its British colonial heritage, America seems to be a democracy that craves Monarchs. The death of John F. Kennedy Junior in a plane crash in July, 1999 brought these longings to the surface of our national rhetoric. 'America's Crown Prince drowns', headlines proclaimed, as if we still had such a thing as crown princes. We were besieged with images of 'John-John' playing at his father's feet under the Presidential desk, and famously, saluting the Presidential casket, as if these images provided the 'ocular proof' of his entitlement to have inherited his father's crown. No matter how much the adult JFK Jr stated his disinclination towards politics (and especially towards the Presidency), Americans thrust his greatness upon him posthumously, speaking of his 'tragic legacy' and 'how lightly he wore his royalty' (Jonathan Alter 1999: 50), as if there were some special Providence in the fall of this sparrow. As tragic as his untimely death was, it revealed more than anything how deeply runs our sentimental desire to behold the stamp of the father in the form of the son.

Phantom Monarchy lives on not only in how we want to see our Magistrates but in the way we nurse our own sense of entitlement to what were once the prerogatives of royalty: life, liberty, and the pursuit of happiness, with the latter increasingly defined as wealth. Even as we demand our 'riches', we refuse to be held responsible for how the political system is actually run. To this extent, Hamlet can certainly be regarded as a new kind of Everyman; or at least as a model of what the new American cyberdream tells us we can all be – *virtual royalty*. If the allure of cloning is the endless perpetuation of self, and the lure of the global stock market is the effortless perpetuation of wealth, what kind of legacy will Americans be able to offer history? The post-millenial Hamlet is already with us – and if we listen carefully we may hear him philosophize, with the same degree of angst that used to be reserved for murdered fathers, thus:

> To buy, or not to buy – that is the question:
> Whether 'tis nobler in the mind to suffer

The slings and arrows of Social Security,
Or to take stock against a sea of troubles,
And by investing end them? To buy, to sell,
And by selling to say we end the heartache
and the thousand natural shocks
That markets are heir to – 'tis a consummation
devoutly to be wish'd: to hold, to trade,
To trade, perchance to regret – Ay, there's the rub
For in regret what dreams may come,
When we have shuffled off our dot.com stock
Must give us pause. There's the respect,
That makes calamity of so long a life.

6

It's the Monarchy, Stupid

It's the economy, Stupid.

– James Carville

I

On June 3, 2002, Queen Elizabeth II celebrated her 'Golden Jubilee Anniversary' commemorating fifty years on the British Throne. In response, the British public expressed an enthusiasm that was astonishing given that only a few years earlier nearly half of all Britons polled agreed with the proposition that England would 'not be worse off' if the monarchy were to be dismantled. After public image damage brought on by years of marital scandal in the royal family and capped by the death of Princess Diana in 1997, the Queen seemed entirely to have recovered her sentimental hegemony. For four days Elizabeth and her entourage took their progress only to experience an 'outpouring of affection' that signalled 'an astonishing upturn in the fortunes of the royal house', a triumph of affirmation that five years ago 'would have seemed starkly inconceivable'.[1] Vernon Bogdanor (2000), a professor of government at Oxford University, concluded from this 'outpouring' that 'the first fifty years of the queen's reign confirm what most of us surely have always understood in our bones, that we remain a profoundly monarchical nation'.

While the use of the royal 'we' in Bogdanor's statement might not go down so well with many non-Anglo-Saxon Britons, he nonetheless articulates a phenomenon that, understood 'in the bones' or not, remains structurally true about a nation that still cannot imagine itself without the institution of monarchy – a nation for which royalty still serves as guarantor of British identity. Perhaps this resurgence of popularity would not have occurred had the beloved Queen Mother not died in the previous year. A figurehead of stout Britishness (and one of the few royals actually to be British), the Queen Mum was the 'people's Queen', suspended in the nostalgic amber of her stalwart Second World War role of morale booster. Despite Tony Blair's elimination of hereditary peerage in the House of Lords, the establishment of regional parliaments in Scotland, Northern Ireland, and Wales, and the demystification of royal life over the last twenty years, such shifts have not yet rendered the pageantry of monarchy insufficient to sustain an institution that funnels staggering wealth to a few Germanic aristocrats who do little of substance to earn their keep.

At stake here, however, is the very notion of what constitutes political 'substance'. Royal apologists argue for the indispensable political power of the symbology itself:

> A constitutional monarchy settles beyond argument the crucial question of who is to be head of state and it places the position of head of state beyond political competition. In doing so . . . it alone is in a position to interpret the nation to itself.[2]

What is being defended in this formula is less the value of monarchy *per se* than the foreclosure of contestation, the safety of things being 'settled beyond argument' and the comfort of knowing 'in the bones' (and therefore not having to know in the mind) that the institution 'places the position of head of state beyond political competition'. But with placement beyond political competition comes the threat of placement beyond political relevance. What does monarchy mean if its national function has been reduced solely to self-exegesis, 'to interpreting the nation to itself'? Bogdanor's articulation assumes that important political issues left to citizen-subjects will inevitably lead to squabbling and consequently to what he sees as the dangerous spectre of an *incorrect self-interpretation*; that left merely to political devices, Britons would find themselves in a position not unlike Shakespeare's weepy queen in *King Richard II*, to whom Richard's flunky Bushy says:

> Each substance of a grief hath twenty shadows,
> Which shows like grief itself, but is not so;
> For sorrow's eye, glazed with blinding tears,
> Divides one thing entire to many objects,
> Like perspectives, which rightly gazed upon,
> Show nothing but confusion... (2.2.14–19).[3]

Arresting British character development at the political 'mirror stage', Bogdanor argues that only the Monarch can reflect the 'substance' of the subject back to himself or herself; only the Monarch can exist beyond the slant of 'perspectives' and see 'one thing entire' (*RII*, 2.2.20). His defence of monarchy suggests that while the Tudor doctrine of the Divine Right of Kings may have been 'crossed out' long ago by 'modernity', its ghostly spectre – what Slavoj Žižek would call the 'indivisible remainder' – persists.

However 'modern' contemporary British monarchy may be, it sustains an ideological fantasy that seems to have remained intact since the seventeenth century. In *We Have Never Been Modern*, Bruno Latour argues that the God of the so-called moderns becomes a casualty of the debates between the subject (political) and object (scientific) poles that discursively organize the 'dialectic of Enlightenment'.[4] According to Latour, God has been 'crossed-out', or, rather, bracketed – since what is involved is a suspension and not an erasure:

> A fourth guarantee had to settle the question of God by removing Him for ever from the dual social and natural construction, while leaving Him presentable and usable nevertheless. Hobbes's and Boyle's followers succeeded in carrying out this task – the former by ridding Nature of any divine presence, the latter by ridding Society of any divine origin.... No one is truly modern who does not agree to keep God from interfering with Natural Law as well as with the laws of the Republic. God becomes the crossed-out God of metaphysics... (1993: 32–3).

The threat the 'Modern Constitution' poses is that each discourse becomes paralysed in the contest to establish the most authoritative hermeneutic for interpreting the 'real world'. In such a scenario, a tiebreaker is sometimes required. While God is suspended by the 'constitution' he remains the implied lynchpin that holds the entire apparatus together. Latour describes the danger of eliminating God entirely from the interpretive picture:

> An overly thorough distancing would have deprived the moderns of a critical resource they needed to complete their mechanism. The Nature-and-Society twins would have been left hanging in the void, and no one would have been able to decide, in case of conflict between the two branches of government, which one should win out over the other (Latour 1993: 34).

Safely stowing the crossed-out God in a 'place beyond political competition' (the realm of metaphysics), the Modern Constitution 'establishes as arbiter an infinitely remote God who is simultaneously totally impotent and the sovereign judge' (ibid.).

By being 'simultaneously totally impotent and the sovereign judge', the crossed-out God can periodically be called back from the void to interpret the nation to itself, much like Bogdanor's contemporary monarch. In fact, we could call Bogdanor's monarch a *crossed-out Monarch*, who – like the crossed-out God – is able to be sovereign judge only by virtue of being totally impotent. One would think that lack of potency would render the monarchy obsolete; but here is the contemporary twist, the one that begins to emerge in the seventeenth century: the political 'castration' of the monarchy seems to have endowed it with power of a different nature. As Edgar Wilson describes it,

> The monarch does not rule, but rather reigns. This important distinction reflects the fact that the monarch exercises no political power. Indeed, the head of state defines a limit to political power...[this] political neutrality, among other things allows the monarch to stabilise the political process...the monarch is consulted by the government, offers encouragement, and urges caution, which is calculated to prevent extreme and disturbing action. The influence exercised by the head of state in this way has tended to increase in proportion to the decrease of effective political power at her disposal (Wilson 1989: 10).

Wilson is correct that the monarch currently does not exercise the 'effective' political power that legislates and administers;

however, 'influence' should never be underestimated as an effective force in its own right. In a media age, whether in the global electronic forms with which we are currently familiar or in 'early modern' forms such as theatre and chronicle history, influence – the symbolic ability to interpret a nation to itself – may be the most potent political force of all.

For most of its long history, the British Crown exercised a direct political power that was, to be sure, increasingly checked as monarchy became more centralized and various offices were created to carry out the more complex regional functions of government. But never before in British history has it been as fully divorced from political power as it is now. This divorce can be seen either as a demotion, insofar as the medieval doctrine of the Divine Right of Kings was designed to suture ruling and reigning in a way that recognized little difference between them, or as a promotion, insofar as the contemporary 'transcendence' of monarchy renders it more potent by virtue of being relieved of its duty to govern. It may be bracketed, but in the latter view, a monarchy untainted by the vulgar mechanisms of daily economic and social administration is also better 'held in reserve' to become entirely sacred or sublime.

Contemporary British monarchy has clearly undergone a sea change; but we can read an earlier version of the crossed-out monarch in the political trauma at the centre of Shakespeare's *Henriad*. What links both historical moments is the way that each posits an increase of influence in direct proportion to a decrease of effective political power at the monarch's disposal. In both scenarios, influence is most willingly embraced as a by-product of maximum impotence. The separation of political and interpretive agencies is a key dilemma in Shakespeare's second tetralogy. In Elizabethan England the offices are fused under the aegis of absolute monarchy, which exercised the 'right' both to power and to interpretation, and which understood in its doctrinal 'bones' that political hegemony resides precisely in the ability to interpret the nation to itself. And yet, a mere fifty years later, England would enter a civil war in which a legitimate king would be tried and executed for crimes against the state. In the emerging political world that the *Henriad* both anatomizes and anticipates, what will it take to establish the Crown in a realm 'beyond political argument'?

II

> Political and cultural weapons are customarily deployed to
> maintain in operation an identity structure which, if laid out as
> doctrine, would be absurd.
>
> – Tom Nairn[5]

In his discussion of Scottish efforts to establish an autonomous
identity, Tom Nairn argues that even before the onset of 'devolution', Scotland had been developing a 'backyard autonomy' in
which the 'backyard' was the realm of civil society rather than of
'organized political dissent' (1997: 204). Civil society, according
to Nairn,

> is essentially a reactive idea. It has arisen and sometimes
> appealed quite widely in exceptional situations or moments of
> crisis, as a way of exorcising a certain type of threat (ibid.: 75).

That threat is of course the danger of open political opposition,
the very 'arguments' that Vernon Bogdanor claims are
prevented or settled in advance by the figure of the monarch.
Whether or not we agree with Nairn that the concept of civil
society is 'essentially a reactive idea' (i.e. conservative), the term –
invented in 1767 by Scottish Presbyterian minister Adam
Ferguson in *An Essay on the History of Civil Society* – usefully maps
the less codified but no less palpable 'institutions' that occupy
the ground between clan and state, tribe and nation, and regime
and 'regime-change'. As Nairn describes it, Ferguson's 'civil
society' is

> the diffuse assemblage of anything and everything which can
> be located somewhere in between politics and state power on
> the one hand, and the family on the other (ibid.: 77).

Diffuse it may be; but those of us who live in contemporary
Britain and America 'know in our bones' that civil society, in this
definition, is the turf on which the majority of our daily social,
material, and psychological battles occur. 'Nobody', says Nairn,
'would deny the existence or significance of such institutions';
and yet,

> In what sense do they compose an overall or corporate entity
> meriting a title like 'civil society'? In what sense are they

self-standing or self-directing as distinct from control by Monarchs, politicians, policeman or administrators? (ibid.: 77).

What holds together any kind of 'corporate entity' is always a tricky question; but in Shakespeare's second history tetralogy, the corporate entity known as the monarchy comes into crisis as 'coalitions of the unwilling' form provisional and temporary insurgencies. Much of *The Henriad* takes place in a 'backyard' in which various autonomies are growing wild, and in which the political and cultural weaponry usually deployed to maintain the doctrinal divisions between monarchs and subjects no longer exercises any influence. The Crown has rule; what it lacks is the capacity to reign.

In the opening scenes of *Richard II*, King Richard's rhetoric of majesty begs the question of how far the practice of a doctrine may be pushed before those subjected to it call its bluff. If, as C.G. Thayer has argued, it is true that 'Shakespeare has most certainly loaded the deck against his Richard ... by following some contemporary doctrines out to their logical conclusions', the more radical implication extends far beyond 'his Richard' to the fact that any doctrine may be imperiled under the right (or wrong) circumstances.[6] Richard's openly provocative behaviour makes the audience, as well as his kinsmen and counsel, wonder whether doctrines should *ever* have logical conclusions.

In the first act of the play, Richard seems oblivious to the political need to secure consent. As legitimate monarch and head of his culture's dominant 'corporate entity', technically he is entitled to disregard others' concerns if he so chooses. Since one of the key functions of any doctrine is to eliminate the need constantly to renegotiate premises, its adoption should render consent irrelevant: there is either compliance or disobedience. Richard's decision to humiliate Mowbray and Bolingbroke, to set up and then abort their duel, his subsequent capricious banishment of both men, and, lastly, his seizure of Bolingbroke's estate upon the death of John of Gaunt are simultaneously represented by Shakespeare as open provocations as well as royal entitlements. Does the problem lie in Richard or in the doctrine of Divine Right? Upon learning in 2.1 of the death of his uncle John of Gaunt, Richard declares that

> The ripest fruit first falls, and so doth he.
> His time is spent, our pilgrimage must be.
> So much for that. Now for our Irish wars.
> We must supplant those rough rug-headed kerns,
> Which live like venom where no venom else
> But only they have privilege to live.
> And, for these great affairs do ask some charge,
> Towards our assistance we do seize to us
> The plate, coin, revenues, and moveables
> Whereof our uncle Gaunt did stand possessed
>   (2.1.154–63).

York's instant and vehement rebuke makes it clear that by seizing Bolingbroke's estate Richard weakens the primogenitory structures that buttress his own position as legitimate king:

> Take Hereford's rights away, and take from time
> His charters and his customary rights;
> Let not to-morrow then ensue to-day;
> Be not thyself – for how art thou a king
> But by fair sequence and succession?
> If you do wrongfully seize Hereford's rights,
> Call in the letters patents that he hath
> By his attorneys general to sue
> His livery, and deny his off'red homage,
> You pluck a thousand dangers on your head,
> You lose a thousand well-disposed hearts,
> And prick my tender patience to those thoughts
> Which honor and allegiance cannot think (195–207).

The sole function of York's speech here is to eliminate any possibility that Richard might be blind to the 'logical conclusions' of his actions. York's sermon, however, seems to fall on deaf ears:

> Think what you will, we seize into our hands
> His plate, his goods, his money, and his lands.

Richard's response is so dismissive that it is tempting to attribute it to petulance and consequently to overlook its ideological complexity. Some critics hear in these lines only a 'stunning obtuseness', one in which Richard misses the point of York's corrective tirade.[7] However, the very 'point' of York's speech is that unless one is the village idiot, it is impossible to miss this point.

Richard's reply is delivered with too much relish merely to be a clueless misstep. No utterance could be more contemptuous than 'think what you will'; but within the frame of Divine Right, the words are a simple declaration of royal fact. What Richard says, technically at least, is not open to dispute: 'It does not matter what you think – I am King and you are not.' But as Northrop Frye has put it,

> In the Middle Ages the effective power was held by the great baronial houses, which drew their income from their own land and tenants, many of them serfs; they could raise private armies...In such a situation a medieval king had theoretical supremacy, but not always an actual one, and as his power base was often narrower than that of a landed noble, he was perpetually hard up for money.[8]

In such a situation – theoretical supremacy on the one hand, lack of effective power on the other – Richard is neither a 'criminal' nor a 'mental defective' (Thayer 1983: 29). We are left then with the dilemma of how properly to understand his 'violations'.

Slavoj Žižek argues that with the emergence of enlightenment democracy as a viable concept,

> the locus of Power becomes an empty place...In pre-democratic societies, there is always a legitimate pretender to the place of power, somebody who is fully entitled to occupy it, and the one who violently overthrows him has simply the status of an usurper, whereas within the democratic horizon, everyone who occupies the locus of Power is by definition a usurper (1991: 267).

Even prior to the 'democratic horizon', Shakespeare understood that the king is ever only a place-holder of the void. However, Shakespeare also knew that, as the cultural 'quilting point', the king is an indispensable place-holder. In Divine Right culture it is imperative that on some final level the king not be held to account, that he not be subject to the same standards that govern other men's behaviour. York's rational argument that Richard's entitlement to power derives from the same system of primogeniture that should protect Bolingbroke's inheritance is in its own way an ideological usurpation, all the more threatening than direct attack precisely because it is so 'reasonable'. York's logic describes a king who, ultimately, is no different from the rest of the nobility and is subject to identical structuring principles.

But if the king is not like other men, he may participate in but cannot be circumscribed by the political system that organizes the lives and property of his subjects. As Ronald R. MacDonald argues, Richard 'takes the extreme position that, if what the language of sacred kingship seems to be saying is really true, if he really is God's anointed, then he should not have to lift a finger to retain his kingdom'.[9] Whether or not the language of sacred kingship is 'really true, the social order is organized around paying lip service to it. More importantly, it derives its political substance precisely from the fact that it is an unreasonable doctrine: sublime irrationality is the only thing that confers monarchy's 'effective' substance.[10]

Consequently, when Richard says 'think what you will' he exhibits a perverse brand of ethical heroism: a ruthless insistence on the zero-sum status of a doctrine that everyone, regardless of where they stand on the 'belief' spectrum, has agreed to abide by. In *The Sublime Object of Ideology*, Žižek describes the 'primal baptism' as a retroactively foundational reconstitution of a subject's substance – in simpler terms, a process in which the attribution of something 'more than itself' to a name, a person, a figure, or a symbol is re-read as originating in the thing itself. Žižek's formulation corresponds to the logic of the commodity fetish:

> 'Being-a-king' is an effect of the network of social relations between a 'king' and his 'subjects'; but – and here is the fetishistic misrecognition – to the participants of this social bond, the relationship appears necessarily in an inverse form: they think that they are subjects giving the king the royal treatment because the king is already in himself, outside the relationship to his subjects, a king; as if the determination of 'being-a-king' were a 'natural' property of the person of a king. How can one not remind oneself here of the famous Lacanian affirmation that a madman who believes himself to be a king is

no more mad than a king who believes himself to be a king –
who, that is, identifies immediately with the mandate 'king'?
(1989: 25).

And yet, if the king does not identify with the mandate 'king',
who will? Richard's behaviour corresponds to the Kantian exercise of the absolute limits of ethics: either monarchy is a 'primal
baptism', as hereditary Divine Right stipulates that it is, or it is
not; either it confers special transcendence on its placeholder or
it is, as York argues quite reasonably, dependent upon a descrip-
tivist system of 'functions'. In a sense, Richard's insistence on his
mandate is an overdue reply to (the now dead) Gaunt's blatant
disrespect in 1.3:

> Richard. Why, uncle, thou has many years to live.
> Gaunt. But not a minute, king, that thou canst give (1.3.217–18).

By referring to Richard with the generic and depersonalized
'king', Gaunt had 'primally unbaptized' him and reminded him
that his status was merely an effect of social relations. The moment
the mandate is openly demystified, the moment the fetishistic
'misrecognition' is abandoned, the constitutive irrationality of
monarchy itself is exposed.

That irrationality is, however, foundational to the entire
enterprise of royal and aristocratic practice; consequently,
York's warning to Richard is absurd because it attempts (to
paraphrase Nairn) to lay out that practice – due inheritance and
succession – as a doctrine, whilst ignoring the 'indivisible
remainder' that endows special entitlement to the throne.
Richard's reply may seem equally absurd, but he does have the
ethical advantage of matching the doctrine to the practice (as
Francis Bacon put it, 'a Prince can do no wrong'). The double-
bind Shakespeare puts Richard in consists of the fact that adher-
ence to principle can look exactly like sociopathic behaviour.
Harry Berger Jr says, 'it is as if [Richard] is daring his audience
to show respect for the kingship and the rituals of authority even
as he demeans them' (1989: 54). And as Barbara Hodgdon notes,
Richard turns kingship 'upside down, speaking its hegemony as the
paradoxical process of its destruction' (1991: 113). Hodgdon's
formulation raises a striking question, one relevant to contemporary

politics as well: What happens to a culture's identity structure if the only way its most powerful institution can 'speak its hegemony' is through the 'process of its destruction'?[11]

Looked at in this light, the drastic transformation Richard undergoes – from the autocrat of the first act to the alternately defiant and weepy storyteller of the third, to the 'poet' of inwardness of the fifth – confirms his structural function as the purveyor, and defender, of the irrational element in sacralized politics. This is something that Shakespeare understood in his bones: the moment any kind of politics is anchored in the 'sacred', irrationality – of one kind or another – is required to maintain its operations. This explains why, paradoxically, the more inconsistent and irrational Richard becomes as the play progresses, the more we come to feel – in spite of ourselves – that he is (in the primally baptized sense), and deserves to be, King.

If Richard 'stands for' the necessary irrational element that sustains the sublime object of Monarchy, then the critical tradition of 'psychologizing' his character misses the point. This becomes increasingly clear by the middle of the play: no matter how ridiculous Richard sounds, someone must believe that the monarch is God's annointed king and it might as well be God's annointed king. Richard's tirade to Aumerle in 3.2. is certainly as embarrassing for the audience as it is for his attendants; but there is method to the rhetorical madness of ruined grandeur:

> So when this thief, this traitor Bolingbroke,
> Who all this while hath revelled in the night
> whilst we were wand'ring the Antipodes,
> Shall see us rising in our throne, the east,
> His treasons will sit blushing in his face,
> Not able to endure the sight of day,
> But self-affrighted tremble at his sin.
> Not all the water in the rough rude sea
> Can wash the balm off from an anointed king.
> The breath of worldly men cannot depose
> The deputy elected by the Lord.
> For every man that Bolingbroke hath pressed
> To lift shrewd steel against our golden crown,
> God for his Richard hath in heavenly pay

> A glorious angel. Then, if angels fight,
> Weak men must fall; for heaven still guards the right
>   (3.2.47–62).

There is nothing 'wrong' with what Richard is saying apart from the fact that it is not true: the stones will not arm, nor troops of angels appear to defend him. None of this is Richard's 'fault' (except insofar as his own political cynicism seems to cut in and out at inopportune moments). Through Richard the erratic individual, Shakespeare is putting sacralized doctrine to a reality test, and it fails miserably.

We should therefore regard Richard neither as a political idiot nor as an 'hysteric' but as a martyr who occupies the privileged position of one who 'tarries with the negative', a figure who pushes to its radical limit the truth-value of a 'sacred' doctrine that organizes a culture's power relations. Richard is a victim – not of Bolingbroke and not of his own character defects but of an historical rupture caused not by fetishistic disavowal but by the disavowal of the constitutive reality of fetishism. His 'self-destructive' behaviour, if read in this way, is constructive on another front: it is an effort to construe the 'absolute' in absolute monarchy.

In his discussion of the 'monism' that is posited as the endpoint of Hegelian dialectics, Žižek argues that the 'One' of that monism is always already split:

> We could say that 'absolute knowledge' implies the recognition of an absolute, insurmountable impossibility: the impossibility of accordance between knowledge and being. Here one should reverse Kant's formula of the transcendental 'conditions of possibility'; every positively given object is possible, it emerges only against the background of its impossibility, it can never fully 'become itself', realize all its potential, achieve full identity with itself. In so far as we accept the Hegelian definition of truth – the accordance of an object with its Notion – we could say that no object is ever 'true,' ever fully 'becomes what it effectively is'. This discord is a positive condition of the object's ontological consistency.[12]

The first three acts of *Richard II* engage the audience in precisely this kind of Hegelian exercise in order to determine to what extent this 'object' (the King) will accord with its Notion (divine annointment). Richard fuses and confuses the Notion with the object; in so doing, he puts the crown into crisis by acting as if he were in his 'being' identical to what he is in doctrine: an absolute monarch. 'We do not destroy an object by mangling it from outside but, quite the contrary, by allowing it freely to evolve its potential and thus to arrive at its Truth' (ibid.: 69). What Shakespeare seems to be proposing in the opening salvo of the *Henriad* is that the notion of divine-right monarchy must be destroyed in practice before its object can (retroactively) accord with its Notion. In other words (to recall Barbara Hodgdon's observation), only through destruction can the king (and the Crown) become a sublime object.

What Bolingbroke and his henchmen do not foresee is that by deposing Richard, they will transform what they themselves regard with pragmatic contempt – the purely symbolic – into the most powerful political category of all; more powerful for being cut off from rational material and economic interests. By substituting external negation for 'internal negation' (Richard's self-undermining), Bolingbroke's actions offer Richard exactly what he needs 'freely to evolve [his] potential and thus to arrive at [his] truth'. With the usurpation, Bolingbroke eradicates the internal contradiction that kept Richard from actually *being* God's anointed king. Attacking Richard's legitimacy from the 'outside', Bolingbroke unwittingly reconstitutes Richard's Divine Election.[13]

Bolingbroke divorces Richard's influence from his effective power in a way that foreshadows contemporary British monarchy. Shakespeare makes it clear that Richard's influence becomes more palpable by virtue of being severed from actual power; and Bolingbroke's 'succession', a pragmatic victory, will forever be a symbolic failure. Cut loose from the 'crudely' material, the symbolic Crown can now operate as pure 'neutrality' or disinterestedness, in a place (to echo Bogdanor) 'beyond political arguments'. And although the two parts of *Henry IV* will be driven by political arguments, a usable crown – the object-in-accord-with-its-Notion – will elude King Henry IV.

With his own actions, Bolingbroke enables Richard to transform himself from the annoying provocateur of the first two acts into the 'beautiful soul', whose logic runs thus:

> The enemy-figure, the Party supposed to impede my fulfilment, is in truth the very precondition of my position of

Beautiful Soul; without it, I would lose the big Culprit, the point of reference to which my subjective position acquires its consistency (Žižek 1991: 71).

The political psychology of the 'beautiful soul' helps us to make sense of Richard's shifts in subjectivity without having to resort to Oedipal psychologizing. When Bolingbroke and Richard are finally brought 'brow to frowning brow', Bolingbroke – a big Culprit if ever there was one – enables Richard to demonstrate

> the famous Lacanian proposition that the speaker receives from the other (his addressee) his own message in its inverted – its true – form. The subject whose activity misfires, who achieves the opposite of what he intended, must gather enough strength to acknowledge in this un-looked for result the truth of his intention. That is to say, truth is always the truth of the symbolic 'big Other' (ibid.: 71–72).

Richard's transformation into the Beautiful Soul is 'the truth of his intention'; although he sounds distressed to be losing his throne, all of his actions have been leading him towards this supremely sacrificial moment.[14]

In the wake of Richard's ethical 'test' to Dirty Harry – 'go ahead, take my crown, make my day' – Bolingbroke's usurpation is not the cause of the play's central rupture but its symptom. The political trauma inaugurated in *Richard II*, and played out in the remainder of *The Henriad*, is not usurpation *per se* but the calamity of being forced, without any mitigation, to confront the truth of what doctrines are designed to do. The real crisis behind the designated crisis of usurpation is the shattering of doctrinal unimpeachability. That rupture results in the sudden expulsion into the scary 'backyard' inhabited by clans, tribes, separate and competing coalitions, a place where 'contracts' cannot be secured, and social relations are entirely subject to that most volatile of all political commodities: continuing consent. In the absence of doctrinal invincibility, everything depends on the less reliable codes of a nascent civil society, which becomes simultaneously more improvisatory and influential. Caught between the rock of Doctrine and a hard place of complete cynicism, politics – like everything else – takes place in the middle. But in Shakespeare's day, the 'middle' cannot hold.

III

In *Richard II*, Bolingbroke does not need 'interiority' because his role is to play Big Culprit to Richard's Beautiful Soul. Shakespeare will not burden Bolingbroke with subjectivity until he becomes King Henry IV; not, in other words, until he tries to leave behind his 'big-culpritness'. Only after he has been crowned does he evince concern about his 'unthrifty son'. He will spend the better part of his eponymous plays trying to disavow the implications of the pragmatism that crowned him and that made his legitimacy impossible. A master opportunist, Bolingbroke exercises 'instrumental reason', which as Hugh Grady argues, is built on the paradox 'that while it works to magnify and enhance the power of its user, it also entraps that very user because its logic works independently of any purely subjective intentions'.[15] Instrumental reason may be what it takes to get a particular job done, but the investments it guarantees – wealth, status, land, plate, revenue, patents, monies – may never openly be articulated as the sole aim of political power without precipitating a crisis in the realm of 'values-discourse'.

When material interests reach the ideological surface of a culture's operations, doctrine begins to sound like what it is – an exercise in individual and collective self-delusion. This is why York's lecture to Richard about 'how the system really works' falls on deaf ears; it lacks the kernel of the irrational, the 'hetero-geneous' element that fills out every ideological fantasy and makes it effective as a social performance.[16] While it is true that the *Henriad* charts a political world that does not yet 'have provisions for democratic elections' (Thayer), Bolingbroke's usurpation and the civil wars it triggers stage a series of *impeachment scenarios* that can only make sense retroactively, from the vantage point of a radical democratic potentiality (one that will become more radical in 1649 with the execution of Charles II). This is *not* to say that Bolingbroke's actions spring from any democratic impulse; but they do achieve the 'first step' in a process that will lead, eventually, to constitutional monarchy and subsequently, to democracy. His actions expose the monarchy as a job that can, and indeed will, be judged on the merits of its execution.

Doctrine alone can no longer guarantee the position. At the same time, 'merit' alone is insufficient; there will have to be some extra-rational substance emanating from the crown that will render its power sublime and its holder 'above the fray'. But now that legitimate succession is no longer enough to generate that 'substance', how is to be produced? The theme of meritocratic deserts – fundamental to later seeds of democracy – runs throughout *The Henriad*, from Falstaff's grandiose belief that his friendship with Hal will be richly rewarded, to Hotspur's refusal to be impressed by Glendower's claims of wizardry, to Williams' challenge to the wisdom of King Henry V's policies. No royal figure in the Shakespearean corpus will make more of a show of meritocracy than 'King Harry'. However cynically it may be launched in *Richard II*, fellow-feeling – the basis of civil society – and not 'absolute' monarchy will be the primary political mechanism to be mastered and moulded into a new corporate entity in *Henry V*.

In his discussion of Benedict Anderson's well-known concept of 'imagined communities', Andrew Murphy says that 'a nation is constituted by acts of imaginative sympathy – a sort of conceptual glue that binds citizens together.'[17] But without an effective ideological framework, 'imaginative sympathy' is impossible. In the first three plays of *The Henriad*, Divine Right is the only available 'conceptual glue' for the 'imagined community' of England, and it will not stick. When Richard is usurped, heterogeneous sacredness is replaced by functional or homogeneous machinery: of mutual obligation, indebtedness, competing claims, and self-interested pragmatisms. King Henry IV turns sacred doctrine into a mechanism; and no mere mechanism will convince people that Bolingbroke is any more 'entitled' to the throne than Harry Percy, Mortimer, or anyone else because mechanisms support modes of production, not modes of belief.[18]

In 'crossing out' Richard, Bolingbroke crossed out God's endorsement without setting up any guarantee for calling it back in to settle the inevitable disputes. If the monarchy 'stabilizes' or 'defines a limit' to the political process, it functions as a Lacanian *point-de-capiton*, the quilting point that anchors disparate and irreconcileable fragments in place. Ernesto Laclau's key insight – that 'Society does not exist' – is nomologically correct insofar as in reality there is no unified Entity called 'Society'; there is only a loose conglomeration of quasi-entities that share unequal access to resources and to social and political assets (Laclau and Mouffe

1989: 97–114 *passim*). Henry IV's real crime, then, is *symbolicide*, with its attendant revelation that 'Monarchy does not exist.' However, as long as there is a 'really existing' legitimate monarch, at least the question of what *kind* of non-existent Society one lives in can be kept at bay.

In the two parts of *Henry IV*, the regionalism that proved so useful to Bolingbroke when he usurped Richard II has taken on a life of its own. 'Parochialism', Nairn reminds us, 'is not just a state of mind but a social structure' (2000: 197), one that works against any united formation unless counteracted by a 'higher' or 'sublime' shared interest that can escape its atavistic pull. As Nairn explains,

> Theorists of nationality-politics have invented the term 'ethnoscape' to describe certain aspects of traditional national identity. By analogy, what we're dealing with here might be called the 'sovereigntyscape' of the United Kingdom – the deeper configuration of central authority inherited and taken for granted, and in practice grafted on to most ideas (including popular ideas) of the nation, of 'what it means' to be British or English (ibid.: 125).

While Nairn is describing contemporary 'devolution' of the United Kingdom, there is not yet a 'Great Britain' in *The Henriad*, nor will there be until the coronation of King James I. What Prince Hal will have to grapple with as Henry V is less his 'right' to inherit the throne from his father than how to reconstitute from the political rubble a 'landscape of sovereignty' (Nairn 2000: 124). King Harry will need to disentangle his inheritance from the grip of a tainted legacy from the past and transform it into a legacy for the future. Shakespeare's *Henry V* anatomizes the political genius required to manufacture a notion of 'Englishness' that will serve *first* as a mechanism to establish an 'ethnoscape' and *then* as a primal baptism to transform that 'ethnoscape' into a 'sovereigntyscape'.

Despite the centuries that separate Shakespeare's crown from the contemporary crown, a few structures (of feeling perhaps) remain, however improbably, intact. Edgar Wilson has argued that the one overarching myth that has sustained British monarchy is 'the idea that the King or Queen personifies one nation' (1989: 11), at the centre of which is understood to be some essential 'Englishness' that holds it all together. The 'English Heartland', as Nairn calls it,

> continues to behave and feel as if Great Britain and its unitary state still existed. The United Kingdom was such a convenience for the English that they seem, perhaps naturally, still disinclined to give it up (Nairn 2000: 15).

As the 'imaginary repository of the national-life force', the crown is dedicated to ensuring the continuity of Britishness – 'survival: in whatever grandeur remains possible' (ibid.: 51).

The contemporary crown, in other words, is dedicated to preserving an 'ethnoscape' that, at least in Shakespeare's corpus, is 'invented' by Henry V. In the infamous St Crispin's day speech before the battle of Agincourt, Harry 'rallies the troops' with a Utopian vision of a future in which every surviving participant in the battle, however mean or base, will share the magically potent symbolic capital of 'fellowship' with the king. The 'conceptual glue' is the ideological fantasy not of the monarch as sublime patriarch but of the monarch as benevolent big brother. 'Harry the King' strikes the mother of all ideological goldmines by reconceiving sovereignty as fraternal *gemutlichkeit*, a structure of feeling that conflates sentimentality with the will to power:

> This story shall the good man teach his son,
> And Crispin Crispian shall ne'er go by
> From this day to the end of the world
> But we in it shall be remembered,
> We few, we happy few, we band of brothers.
> For he today that sheds his blood with me
> Shall be my brother; be he ne'er so vile,
> This day shall gentle his condition (4.3.57–64).

The soldiers may, as Donald Hedrick has argued, find themselves 'disadvantaged in the present'; but King Harry is not interested in the present (since the spectre of Richard II continues to loom over that memoryscape).[19] Rather, he promises each soldier a share of a legacy that will be delivered to them by the future, a share in the Nation-Thing (Žižek 1993: 201). Henry does, as Hedrick says, maximize 'patriotism through memory' (2003: 473); but it is memory from the future that he promises, not memory of the past.

Instead of presenting himself as the 'repository of the national life force', Henry V constructs an English Nation as a future repository. As Žižek has argued, what creates the desire to 'defend our way of life' cannot be reduced to rational propositions or to ideological values. It requires 'a relationship toward the Nation qua Thing', a recognition of the 'unique way a community organizes its *enjoyment*' (cf. Žižek 1993: 200–5). The Nation-Thing is contradictory, as Žižek points out – its enjoyment can only be experienced by imagining an outside threat, an Other who wants to steal 'our way of life' (what Žižek calls the 'theft of enjoyment' [ibid.]). 'Our way of life' is not, in other words, an ideological cause but rather, something radically contingent that is retroactively transformed (always in opposition to an alien Other) into our 'special substance', our unique way of being, what we imagine to be our collective singularity, our national *jouissance* ('The Power of Pride').

With King Harry's success in creating 'the Nation-Thing', Shakespeare suggests that while a throne inherited legitimately is always preferable, it is not necessary as long as influence is managed cleverly. Harry understands that reigning is more powerful than ruling, and especially when one's campaign is directed towards *regular guys* whose 'limbs were made in England'. 'Made in England' becomes the stamp of pride, an 'Englishness' home grown from the maternal dirt of this 'demi-paradise'. As Terence Hawkes points out,

> Englishness receives its final polishing in the play and enlistment in that crudely engrossing concept is repeatedly urged on and required of the army that Henry leads. Appropriating Scottishness, Irishness and Welshness, its project can be said to present itself, not as a set of distinctive cultural and linguistic features, so much as a kind of fundamental 'reality' that underlies sophisticated notions of difference. It constitutes the basis of that complete and discrete 'world' that the 'British' project set out to create.[20]

By hinting at a 'fundamental reality' that exists between these men whose blood is 'fet from fathers of warproof', the enduring significant differences of Irishness, Scottishness, and Welshness are subsumed beneath a Greco-genotype of 'so many Alexanders'.

'Englishness' in *Henry V* may be only a 'crudely engrossing concept', as Hawkes says. But over time it will become an increasingly sophisticated one, as the durability of the British monarchy proves. In *The Henriad* (and especially in *Henry V*), 'Englishness' serves less as a reification of Nation and more as a triage unit, a temporary repository of the 'national life force' that had hitherto been embodied in the individual figure of the King. 'Harry the king' knows that all monarchs are sitting ducks. By diversifying his stock of symbolic capital, by turning the crown into a kind of mutual fund whose shareholders include his brothers, fellow nobles, and even those base yoemen that 'hath a noble lustre' in their eyes, Harry redistributes royal agency in ways that will make it difficult to target him should things go wrong. If the 'noble English' hold the effective power, as Harry's Crispian's Day speech suggests that they do, he can occupy the politically safer position of wielding influence. After all, it takes an army to raze a village.

This brings us back to Queen Elizabeth and her Golden Jubilee. The homeliness of the Queen, her personal *habitus* of restraint and modesty, perfectly underwrites the castrated power of the Crown; which in turn guarantees that its influence will continue to be indispensable, at least for the foreseeable future, to the notion of 'Britishness'. In spite of its present 'honorific and toothless formalism' (Kastan 1999), the English Crown remains one of the most visible and durable symbols of 'sublime' hereditary aristocracy still standing in the western world. A less visible version, however (one with big teeth), is alive and living across the pond, busy 'defending' its own Nation-Thing abroad, and its special interests at home.

IV

Americans sometimes regard the political 'double-consciousness' of the United Kingdom's constitutional monarchy as charmingly quaint: a hereditary monarch who resides above politics as 'head of state' and a Prime Minister and Parliament mired in politics that actually run the state. I would suggest, however, that double-consciousness is preferable to the 'enlightened false consciousness' that currently afflicts the American presidency. However contradictory British government may seem to Americans, it has the virtue of not operating in direct conflict with its own ideological agenda. Britain, a nation that fetishizes monarchs, at least has a monarchy. America, built on strident rejection of monarchy and hereditary advantage, is not nearly as honest.

Most Americans understand 'in their bones' that George W. Bush would never have obtained the office of President had his father not preceded him. Such an 'inheritance' was triply overdetermined: first by the patronym, second by the position held by the father and third by the father's ability to appoint Supreme Court Justices who would later ratify the son's claims. In the aftermath of the terrorist attacks of September 11, and the quagmire created in Iraq by the American unilateral invasion (and the proliferation of terrorism partly as a result of that invasion), the Clinton presidency is gradually being effaced from our national memory, as is the disputed outcome of the 2000 election. Events have made it possible almost to forget that there was an eight-year Clinton presidency that 'intervened' between Bush *pere* and Bush *fils*. With the return to Iraq, George W. Bush became essentially a direct successor to his father.

Many journalists and scholars have referred to Bush as America's version of Shakespeare's Prince Hal, and many have noted Henry IV's advice to his son to 'busy giddy minds / With foreign quarrels, that action hence borne out / May waste the memory of the former days' (*2 Henry IV*, 4.3. 341–3). Then, as now, there is nothing as effective as picking foreign quarrels to deflect attention away from lingering questions about legitimacy. Like Hal's playing to the masses, Bush's post 9-11 strategy was to further 'identify down' by effacing all signs of class difference between himself and 'hardworking men and women'. The cowboy hat was traded for a hard-hat as he stood shoulder to shoulder with the firemen at 'Ground Zero', the site of the World Trade Center rubble. This celebration of the 'working man' (like Bush's pretense of being a blue-collar Texan) played directly into the strategy of American *noblesse oblige*. At the very moment that firemen and policemen (and now, of course, soldiers) were held up as the apex of American display-identity, the Bush administration was helping, through its economic and social policies, to cement into place what economist and historian Kevin Phillips has called 'millennial plutographics'.

In *Wealth and Democracy: A Political History of the American Rich* (2002), Phillips lays out the plutographics that are currently operating at full pitch in the United States. The US, 'long shed of its revolutionary outlook', has become 'as the new millennium unfolded... home to greater economic inequality than any other major Western nation, including erstwhile aristocratic France and Britain'.[21] Data compiled from the World Bank reveal that the top quintile in the United States make eleven times more money than those at the bottom, a higher wealth discrepancy than in the United Kingdom at a ratio of 9.6, Germany at 5.8, or Japan at 4.3 (ibid.: 124). Nearly half of this wealth is not first generation; *Forbes'* annual lists of wealthiest Americans and their families have the familiar Vanderbilts, Phipps, Rockefellers, and Mellons, along with scions of more recent dynasties, Walton, Bass, Murdoch, Schwab, and Hearst. Dynastic wealth and its extensive reach into American politics is alive and thriving. As Phillips puts it in *The Nation*,

> Politically, we already have a dynasty at 1600 Pennsylvania Avenue: the first son ever to take the presidency just eight years after it was held by his father, with the same party label. This dynasticism also has its economic side: both Bushes, *pere et fils*, having been closely involved with the rise of Enron, another first for a presidential family.... If we lack an official House of Lords, there are Bushes, Tafts, Simons, Rockefellers, Gores, Kennedys and Bayhs out to create a kindred phenomenon.[22]

Of course it is the very 'unofficial' nature of our *de facto* House of Lords that shelters its power and permits it ever more imperious leverage over the political system.

Britain was forced to recognize 'the problem of aristocracy' (Nairn, 2000: 67). The focused economism of the Thatcher regime pushed market forces to the top of the ideological pecking-order, and new power allegiances did not continue to fall along hereditary lines. Given this shift in alliances, as Nairn argues, 'it would simply be ridiculous for any new-style hegemony to try and co-exist with the world's outstanding reliquary of feudalism. The national theme-park implications would be intolerable' (Ibid.: 67).[23] The problem with aristocracy in America, however, is precisely the opposite: not enough attention has been called to its operations (although the flooding of

New Orleans in August 2005, and its graphic illustration of racial and class inequity, may finally change that). There is no 'House' or branch of Congress named for our magnates, yet they exercise inordinate powers of interference. The Senate and the House of Representatives have a shadow rival, the Hall of Pluto-crats: unelected but staggeringly wealthy figures and corpora-tions that wield direct power over who gets into political offices and what they do once they get there.

American plutocrats understand well the importance of severing political process from its formalization; they know that what weakened the British aristocracy was its visibility, and its ongoing and openly divisive use of honorific titles such as Lords, Dukes, Queens, Princes, Kings. Cynical idealists nearly all, American aristocrats know very well that although American doctrine is Democracy (and its implied equal opportunities), it must not be pushed to its logical conclusions. If we were to lay out our doctrine as an actual practice, those who are not obscenely wealthy might be able to exercise some direct political influence, as well as some real power.

In July of 1776, American colonies declared themselves an independent nation by rejecting the policies and privileges of British monarchy and, by extension, of inherited right. Now, several hundred years later, the twenty-first-century United States is not only 'the world's richest major nation' but 'has also become the West's citadel of inherited wealth. Aristocracy [is] a cultural and economic fact, if not a statutory one' (K. Phillips, 2002: 124). America denominalizes its aristocracy: after all, our Constitution (Article 1, Section 9) states that 'No Title of Nobility shall be granted by the United States'. They are called something different here: as George W. Bush has (for once) perfectly put it, 'the haves and the have-mores'. The sublime object of Democracy is individual 'freedom', 'equality', and the injunction to 'Choose!'; the sublime object of Monarchy is 'freedom' from choice, hierarchy, and the transcendence of the collective 'national life force'. Perhaps we should ask ourselves whether the dreamwork of America more closely resembles monarchy than democracy. Our national theme may be demo-cracy, but when push comes to shove (and it has come to shove), it's the Monarchy,....

7
Operation Enduring Hamlet

The name of America's just war on terrorism is 'Operation Enduring Freedom.'

— Ari Fleischer, November, 2001

I

In the final scene of *Hamlet*, the dying prince begs his beloved friend Horatio,

> If thou didst ever hold me in thy heart,
> Absent thee from felicity awhile,
> And in this harsh world draw thy breath in pain
> To tell my story (5.2.351–4).

Hamlet's last wish is that Horatio 'report [his] cause aright', lest his name be wounded in the ignorant ear of 'this harsh world'. This seems a straightforward enough request from one friend to another – 'to tell my story'. But its simplicity is deceptive, coming from a figure whose most famous claim is to 'have that within which passeth show' (1.2.85), a figure who declares that no one, presumably not even Horatio, can 'pluck out the heart of [his] mystery' (3.2.336). Throughout the play Hamlet has expressed interest only in how his father shall be remembered; consequently this deathbed desire for transparency – a last-minute obsession with how his own story will be told – is out of character and signals a change in the play's representational register. Something happens to the prince as he inhabits what Jacques Lacan calls *l'entre deux mortes*, the 'space between two deaths', a space in which Hamlet can say while still alive, and without paradox, 'I am dead Horatio'. The gap between physical death and one's final inscription in the symbolic order is, in Lacan's formulation, where repressed desires can finally materialize, since 'the game is over' and the subject no longer has anything to gain (or lose) by confronting them.[1]

If we believe what Hamlet tells us in his many soliloquies, we would expect that the achievement of revenge upon his father's murderer is the consummation of his 'desire', or at least of the only desire he has expressed in the play. And yet, as he lies dying, Hamlet discovers that he too wants to be remembered, wants to claim an identity that will stand at the centre of its own story rather than being merely ancillary to someone else's (his father's). In the play's closing lines, then, we see what makes *Hamlet* the most formally peculiar of Shakespeare's plays: the irreducible tension between the play's notorious psychological 'interiority' and the crude requirements of the revenge-tragedy genre for a plot that can be bequeathed to narrative history.

Hamlet's dying plea poses an enormous problem, however, not just for Horatio but for the audience as well: How exactly are we to convert our experience of *Hamlet* the play, with its endless mucking about in the filial unconscious, into *Hamlet* the *story*, a narrative in which describable things happen? What at first glance looks like a simple charge to Horatio is, I would argue, no less than a mandate that the audience change generic registers: in effect, that we disavow most of the play we have just seen in order to embrace another version, a 'story' commissioned by the prince himself, to be delivered by Horatio to the ears of posterity.

The longest of Shakespeare's plays, *Hamlet* excruciatingly thematizes its own slow-motion plot. Whatever 'action' occurs merely punctuates a miasma of interiority-discourse generated by the prince, who spends most of the play wallowing in ambivalence and self-loathing. The audience, and not Horatio, witnesses these soliloquys: Horatio speaks with Hamlet only during his more rare moments of resolution. Consequently, Horatio's 'story' of Hamlet will necessarily look very different from Shakespeare's play. In his preview to Fortinbras, Horatio asks leave to

> ... speak to th'yet unknowing world
> How these things came about. So shall you hear

> Of carnal, bloody, and unnatural acts,
> Of accidental judgements, casual slaughters,
> Of deaths put on by cunning and forced cause;
> And, in this upshot, purposes mistook
> Fall'n on th'inventors' heads. All this can I
> Truly deliver (5.2.324–31).

But is Horatio describing the play we've just seen, or something else entirely? Neatly compressed into five lines, Horatio promises to deliver no less than the world's first 'action' *Hamlet*, a version in which the prince is tricked out as a decisive and righteous heir deprived of his throne by a murderous uncle. We must credit Horatio, then, with formulating the first 'Cliff's Notes' version of *Hamlet*, one in which students who might be tested about the play's 'plot' will get only, as Hamlet puts it, 'the occurents more and less / Which have solicited' (5.2–3.362–3).

Of course Horatio can only provide 'upshot' since he has not seen or heard much else; but for the audience, hearing the play's vast labyrinth of introspection boiled down to 'occurents more and less' reinforces just how little plot-time actual *events* have taken. If this is the story Horatio will tell and 'the rest is silence', we might legitimately ask what need then that mountain of discourse, from Hamlet's monologues to Claudius's anguished attempt at confession, from Polonius's sententious editorializing to Ophelia's mad ramblings? What is the value of having witnessed Hamlet's discursive interiority if *none of it* will make its way into 'his story'? Why does the play that virtually models the theory of the 'unconscious' for both Freud and Lacan end 'in a desperate [bid for] the transparency of consciousness'?[2]

To ask these questions is not to fail to appreciate the human suffering the play represents but to raise a serious question about the cultural *afterlife* of a text: what an audience is expected to take away from the theatre and how certain elements in a work give directional thrust to its journey into posterity. If the 'essence' of Hamlet resides in what he thinks and feels when he is not 'acting', a Hamlet for Horatio's action narrative must be, literally, someone else. Is Horatio's 'trailer' to Fortinbras simply a convenient way for Shakespeare to send his audience off knowing how to advertise to friends and neighbours the play 'bounded in a nutshell' (2.2.254)? Or is Shakespeare imagining a different kind of post-play identity for his most famously 'inward' of characters? To what extent will Horatio's action-Hamlet develop, over the *longue durée*, a separate, and even autonomous, existence from his 'true originall copie'? Is it possible that with *Hamlet*, Shakespeare himself is raising the bar on efforts to transform the quagmire of subjective experience into something socially and historically transmissable?

The play closes by issuing a call for the 'story' of Hamlet the prince. The success of this story – the extent to which it 'takes' – will come to constitute what we might think of as the play's historical legacy: what it generates beyond its diegesis and how culturally viable that 'post'-production becomes. As a revenge tragedy that sets up a zero-sum game – the eventual death not only of all its major characters but of Denmark itself – *Hamlet* is in fact a paradigm of failure. Revenge is ultimately taken, but is entirely unproductive within the world of the play, and comes at a cost extreme by any measure. However, if we honour the prince's last wish and make the generic leap from drama to narrative, it becomes possible to view *Hamlet* not as a play about everything leading up to the horizon of a 'revenge event' but as an extended meditation about everything that will lead *away* from it: how post-revenge stories get told and everything they leave out – everything that cannot be encoded within the straitjacket of calendar time. For the fact of the matter is that the most famous revenge tragedy in the history of the English language is a play about subjective destitution and epistemological mortification, conditions friendly neither to edifying narrative nor to 'providential' history.

In a sense, then, we can regard most of Acts 1–4 (the acts that occur before Claudius is slain) as an *anti-history* play, that is to say, as representing those affects, thought processes, doubts, and internal fragmentations that cannot be told or passed along in story form: everything that occupies what I have earlier called affective time.[3] Unlike calendar time, affective time is highly recursive; it never simply marches forward. Re-framed in the logic of affective time, the first four acts of *Hamlet* are concerned not with revenge *per se*, with its ineluctible movement towards a predetermined act of violence, but with the protagonist's relationship to the idea of *having to be a revenger in a revenge tragedy*, with all the indecisions (and the visions and revisions) that a minute may reverse. One could argue that Act 5 is where the actual revenge play proper begins. There are of course 'events' in the earlier acts that will be mentioned in Horatio's story – the murder of the old King, the ghost's appearance, Rosencrantz and Guildenstern's betrayal, the deaths of Polonius and Ophelia; but the whole, huge, vast 'rest' of it will not be represented in Horatio's story; 'the rest', Hamlet says rightly, 'is silence'.

Horatio was not witness to what was inside Hamlet's mind, as we the audience were; nor was he present when Hamlet had his exchanges with Ophelia and Gertrude. Since most of the play's affective material will inevitably be missing from Horatio's version, he is faced with a formidable challenge: assembling for posterity a 'local reading' out of the play's few 'occurants, more and less'. This makes Horatio something akin to the play's resident new historicist: a critical reconstructionist who, because he has no 'objective' or direct access to it, must necessarily leave out of his reconstruction all the irrational complexity and indeterminacy – what Ernesto Laclau calls 'the absent fullness of society' – that always constitute the vast, if hidden, truth behind any history.[4]

The process of creating a history is never about telling the story of what 'really happened' but rather about 'how a particular content succeeds in displacing another content as a stand-in for the Universal' (Žižek, 2000: 179). How does it succeed in the displacement? According to Laclau, by securing hegemonic 'readibility', by enabling 'engaged individuals...more effectively to organize their life-experience into a consistent narrative. Of course, 'readibility' is not a neutral criterion, it depends on ideological struggle' (ibid.: 179). Reducing 'readibility' to 'ideological struggle', however, fails to explain a phenomenon that seems to me more deeply driven by a culture's *libidinal* imagination – by what it *desires and fears* – than by what it believes. As we all know, desire and belief are rarely identical and their respective agendas may even be mutually antagonistic.

A better way to describe what constitutes hegemonic 'readibility' would be *managed meconnaissance* or misrecognition: an ideological fantasy that sifts events through the filters of shared communal desires and identifications. Through managed misrecognition, a culture mobilizes *libidinal*, as well as ideological, investments in a particular version of 'life experience'. These libidinal investments have more to do with cultural self-images than with objective events; they may even reframe events within structures of feeling that may be entirely inappropriate. Stored, so to speak, in what Paul Veyne has called 'the historical unconscious' are all the discredited tropes, desires, and modes of communal affect that do not necessarily obey the dictates of modernity, and that contemporary culture often finds itself compulsively rehearsing in spite of its pretensions to political 'enlightenment'. If History is the province of calendar time, with its intrinsic positivism, then the historical unconscious is where affective time, with its stubborn refusal to relinquish unacceptable desires, holds court.

The separation of the 'absent fullness of society' from the ordering and cataloging of events can only be accomplished by a social agreement, however tacit, to read one's own experience differently than one has experienced it. According to political philosopher Jon Elster, 'The 'decision value' of an experience may...differ from its inherent value'.[5] To privilege an ending based on decision value is retroactively to recalibrate everything that led up to it in accordance with a particular decision *having been* made (or a particular outcome achieved). Decision value strongly influences the production of a history of any kind, cultural or individual – once outcomes are in place, ideological 'quilting points' are retroactively imposed to anchor the narrative.[6] Decision value designates causes on the basis of effects and intentions on the basis of outcomes.

In the case of *Hamlet*, we must ask ourselves whether the decision value of Hamlet's ultimate killing of Claudius is potent enough to make us willing to revise what we have seen. For it is solely on the outcome that Horatio promises to translate the slapdash and occasionally accidental carnage of the play into deliberative intentions prosecuted in the name of justice. *If* the decision value is strong enough, *if* Horatio's brief manual on 'How to Read *Hamlet*' manages successfully to shape centuries of cultural reception, then Horatio becomes the most historically influential figure in the play; and Hamlet – who curses spite that he was born to set things right, who does not want to play the revenger, and who never evinces a desire to be king – becomes someone who, as Fortinbras says, 'was likely, had he been put on / To have prov'd most royal' (5.2.402–3).

British culture has tended to privilege Hamlet the tortured intellectual while Americans prefer Horatio's action-Hamlet. This may have to do with cultural differences in how Britons and Americans think about what constitutes individual 'character' and its relative importance to history. Many if not most Americans outside the academy are repelled by intellectualism and as a rule do not like public figures who prove too knowledgeable or who consider all sides of an issue before taking a position. This anti-intellectualism and distrust of subtle philosophizing are clear in the American preference for 'men of action', even when their actions involve appalling collateral damage. On the whole, Americans disdain soul searching; revision, refinement, and meditation have always been regarded, in the American heart of hearts, as forms of weakness.

The Hamlet who expresses skepticism about the ghost's disclosure breaks one of our cardinal rules: he doubts the command of the authoritative Father. His intellectual constitution requires him to gather other kinds of evidence; although he loathes Claudius, he still has scruples about procedures. This is not a Hamlet to satisfy an American sense of justice, which in the American *libidinal* imagination at least is inseparable from the swift action of revenge. Hamlet's dying desire to be transformed by Horatio's story into someone else matches the American tendency to want to translate messy complexity into 'decision value', even, at times, *before* decisions have been made (for instance, to announce 'Mission Accomplished' before it has been). Let us say then that the sulking, fussy, sexually squeamish and introspective Hamlet of the first four acts belongs to the British, while the Hamlet who finally emerges in Act 5 has emigrated to America. That thing of darkness we acknowledge ours.

II

> My job is to protect America.
>
> – George W. Bush

Early in the 2000 presidential campaign, journalists trotted out the 'War of the Roses' as a conceit to describe the political battle between George W. Bush and Al Gore Jr, both patronymic scions of political dynasties. Several commentators, most notably

William Safire, Judith Shulevitz, and Nicholas Kristof, referred in their columns to Bush as Prince Hal, former 'mad wag' who spent his youth drinking, running around with fraternity friends, and failing adequately to meet his business responsibilities. Shulevitz in the *New York Times* pointed out that the political factor that drove Henry V's pursuit of foreign wars was the need to deflect attention from the civil wars which his father's seizing of the English crown had triggered. Noting that Bolingbroke's usurpation of Richard II posed 'a grave constitutional question', she offers only the coyest of hints that any of this might be 'relevant' to our current political situation.[7]

But of course it is relevant in deeply structural ways that superficial journalistic analogies almost always ignore. Most pervasive among these structures is America's apparent inability or unwillingness, after 230 years, to purge itself of the desire for phantom monarchs, despite its vehemently avowed belief in the principles of a non-hereditary, post-primogenitory politics. Like his quondam counterpart Prince Hal, no president in living memory came to the position under more questionable circumstances than George W. Bush. Since less than half of the American electorate bothers to vote at all, and since Bush lost the popular election by nearly half a million votes, the one indisputable *fact* to come out of 'Indecision 2000' was that the United States (like a monarchy) had a president whom the vast majority of individual citizens did not elect.

But here the *Henry V* analogy ends; for while Bush's 'election' was questionable, his father's was legitimate. If we want to uncover a more compelling, if not compulsive, logic to the current situation, we must look to *Hamlet*. In the immediate aftermath of the Supreme Court decision, George W. Bush, momentarily at least, was more like Claudius, who 'popp'd in between th' election' (5.2.65) and Al Gore's hopes. Gore, briefly to be sure, became Hamlet – a rightful heir who suffered a throne lost to an illegitimate usurper. Annoyingly cerebral, with a condescending insistence on nuance and lengthy monologues, Gore was not the version of Hamlet Americans wanted to see. Gore was the 'British' Hamlet, puffed up with self-rightous outrage and more than ready to whinge about it. Told by a sneering Bush administration to cast off his inky cloak ('just get over it'), he sulked and performed the politician's equivalent of putting on an 'antic disposition': he grew a beard. Even those who voted for Gore felt that stigma had attached to the exiled prince and could not help but blame him for letting himself be deprived of a throne that could so easily have been his, and by a Satyr to his intellectual Hyperion.

Meanwhile, many Americans quickly found themselves ready to revise the experience of 'Indecision 2000' according to its 'decision value' (even *prior* to the 9-11 attacks, many people said 'let's just move on'). It did not take long for Americans to mobilize their signature practice of retroversive history, in this case aided by the fetish our democracy has for sons who inherit their fathers' thrones (think of all the references to the late JFK Jr as 'America's Crown Prince'). George W. Bush, under conditions that can only be described as ludicrous, was almost immediately embraced as the new 'Commander in Chief'.

This was more, however, than just a marriage of convenience between the *fait accompli* and *amor fati*. It was much easier for Bush to tap into the historical unconscious than it should have been; and to understand that, we have to return to the collective libidinal investment – that 'scandalous dimension' – that I described earlier. This investment, disavowed but never dismissed, establishes the pre-conditions out of which a particular history will unfold (for example, it took all of the libidinal intensities of post-Weimar Germany to 'fill out' a mediocre Adolf Hitler with imperial power). A culture's libidinal imaginary is more influential than particular individuals can ever be, no matter how charismatic or well-connected they are; and here is where Raymond Williams' famous phrase 'structures of feeling' proves its perennial usefulness. The same structures of feeling mobilized over the last ten years by films such as *Pearl Harbor* and *Saving Private Ryan*, and books such as Stephen Ambrose's *Band of Brothers* and Tom Brokaw's *The Greatest Generation*, had already primed the affective pump for Bush's reception: the same conditions that were re-enshrining Second World War nostalgia were quietly but insistently making it possible for this undistinguished 'legacy' candidate to ascend to the presidency in the face of a negative popular vote.

Nostalgia and sentimentality require the strip-mining of complexity; and George W. Bush offered the Simplicity of the subject seemingly transparent to itself: a simple mind, simple tastes, and a simple agenda, organized around 'love of country and family'. His very ignorance of politics seemed less a liability than a deployable gift of 'artful stupefaction': a condition, according to Peter Sloterdijk, in which one is simultaneously 'naive and cunning' (1987: 30). As Sloterdijk argues, 'to be an heir always carries a certain 'status cynicism' with it, as is well known from stories about the inheritance of family capital' (ibid.: 6). Repeating the 'integrity of character' mantra ceaselessly throughout his first presidential campaign, Bush used it effectively enough to occlude an alchoholic past, rumors of a youthful fondness for cocaine, an arrest record for drunken driving, several failed and shady business ventures, and a glaring lack of international *savoir faire*.

Unlike Prince Hal, who as Henry V wanted nothing more than to make his subjects forget the perturbed reign of his father, George W. Bush could not wait to resurrect the reign of his, installing Dick Cheney, Donald Rumsfeld, and Colin Powell in key administrative positions. For a nation still reeling from the humiliations of the Clinton impeachment, this good son so obviously honouring the memory of his father was welcome enough to eclipse other doubts about worthiness, expertise, or even legality. From 1998 through the first half of 2001, Americans had become the butt of the world's political jokes – between Bill Clinton's sexual hijinks, the impeachment disgrace, and the embarrassment of Indecision 2000, Americans were ripe for a recovery of dignity as a nation. Starved for a new story to tell about themselves, one 'unmixed with baser matter', they ran to embrace the promises Bush made about his Character; the claims, in Sloterdijk's words, 'that the ego knows itself better than anyone else does and is master of the rules of its own exercise of reason' (1987: 51).

Our choice to accept Bush's performance was neither 'false consciousness' (Marx), nor was it 'structuring structures reproducing structured structures' (Bourdieu), nor 'ideological interpellation' (Althusser). No one was duped. Just as in *Hamlet* the Court freely goes along with Claudius's installation of himself as the new king, everyone in America knew that Bush lost the popular vote; everyone knew a Supreme Court stacked by his father decided the issue; everyone knew he was a wealthy aristocrat and not a 'regular guy'; and everyone knew about the massive disenfranchisement of Florida voters, especially African Americans. *It did not matter*. We knew 'perfectly well what we were doing, but still we were doing it' (Žižek 1989). Ideology critique, with its tacit assumption of the idiot-subject, found itself impotent in the face of all this knowledge. With a logic immune to deconstruction, George W. Bush's historical moment had already arrived with a sentimental melody, even before it would re-arrive with a Big Bang.

What no one could have anticipated during the first year of the Bush reign was that soon he would not only usurp Gore's throne but would also coopt his role as Hamlet.[8] With the terrorist attacks of September 11, 2001, George W. Bush was born again, this time as the 'good' action-Hamlet: ready to take on a time out of joint and *thanking spite that he was born to set things right*. Even as he grieved with the rest of us, he seemed positively elated to discover his destiny. If we were a bit uneasy about all the 'Wanted: Dead or Alive' rhetoric, at least we could now regard it as an example of what Timothy Bewes calls 'instrumental stupidity':

> a manifestation of ignorance adopted willfully, for pragmatic reasons, in order to maximize the rhetorical impact of subjectivity and the potency of individual volition (1997: 105).

September 11 transformed Bush into the Hamlet Americans have always wanted to see – a man more than willing to take arms against a sea of troubles and by opposing, end them. No self-reflective paralysis, no philosophizing here (how some imagine Gore would have responded to 9-11) – just a Supreme Subject with absolute 'potency of individual volition'. This is the figure that Shakespeare's play never delivers, but that Horatio's story has always tantalizingly promised us, if we can just (like Bush) clear away the brush: *a Hamlet unburdened by an unconscious* – the inspiration for every Mad Max, Dirty Harry, Lethal Weapon, and Terminator who 'hangs tough' and never doubts his convictions or his calling.

In the weeks following the attacks, journalists searched images of George W. Bush's face, and seemed to find there

> An eye like Mars to threaten and command,
> A station like the herald Mercury
> New-lighted on a heaven-kissing hill;

> A combination and a form indeed
> Where every god did seem to set his seal
> To give the world assurance of a man (*Hamlet*,
>   3.4.57–62).

They noted with approval his new grey hairs, furrowed brow, and the dark undereye circles that for the rest of us betoken middle age but in this context could only mean sleepless nights of gritty determination. Gone was the signature smirk; reporters noted 'a new seriousness', a 'maturity' as Bush seemed to become capable of understanding even the details of his daily briefings.

With September 11, the nation, like Hamlet, 'wiped away all trivial fond records' about the election; and the Bush administration began its all-out campaign of 'cynical idealism' – a campaign in which free speech is un-American and anyone who dares to criticize the president is 'aiding the terrorists' (John Ashcroft). While no one would say that the 9-11 attacks were anything other than monstrous, the ease and speed with which the Bush administration was able to impose the Patriot Act and the rest of its authoritarian agenda suggests that in a *purely structural way* Osama bin Laden came along as a hideous reply of the Real to something in America's historical unconscious: its unenunciated but palpable demand for *a new national story*, one in which we could again be regarded as the world's heroes.[9] Obviously no American wanted a story like the one Al Quaeda delivered; but there is little doubt that a demand was already taking shape for many months before September 11, the outlines of which were legible in the misty-eyed longing for the fantasmatic purity of the Greatest Generation and the honour they brought to the country.

Let me be completely clear: to say this is *not in any way* to say that America invited the attacks; but it is to suggest that after the extreme national divisions revealed by the Clinton impeachment and, subsequently, by Election 2000, only an eruption of intense hatred against a collective 'us' could unite, 'requilt', a national image tattered during the long farce that constituted the end of the millennium in American politics. And although no one believes that Bush was anything other than horrified by the terrorist attacks, no one can dispute the enormous political benefits it conferred upon his presidency. Before September 11, 2001 his poll ratings were dismal; in the weeks and months that followed, they skyrocketed. On one morning of obscene carnage, Osama bin Laden handed George W. Bush his legitimacy on a silver platter, playing the role of Big Culprit (the Evil One) to Bush's 'Beautiful Soul'.

In the year following the September 11 attacks, however, Bush's aura of being annointed by God 'to rid the world of the Evildoers' began to erode as Osama bin Laden proved too elusive for the war on terror. A detour was required, one that would fruitfully exploit the widespread patriotism that terrorism had provoked. To mobilize this, Bush would have to return to what has always been his fallback position – the Inheritor. As if the crimes committed on his watch were not sufficient, he turned 'back' to crimes committed against his father in his days in office. As Derrida says about Hamlet in *Specters of Marx*,

> One never inherits without coming to terms with some specter, and therefore with more than one specter...That is the originary wrong, the birth wound from which he suffers...that time is 'out of joint' is what is also attested by birth itself when it dooms someone to be the man of right and law only by becoming an inheritor, redressor of wrongs, that is, only by castigating, punishing, killing (1994: 21).

Originarily secondary – even, like Hamlet, in name – George Bush Jr is 'destined to inherit', to castigate, punish, and kill. The spectre in this case, of course, is the *revenant* of Saddam Hussein: as Bush put it so poignantly, 'the guy tried to kill my Dad'. While Bush was from the beginning an 'inheritor', from his 'legacy admission' to Yale to his too easy entrance into politics, only after September 11 did he become what Derrida calls *the right kind of inheritor*, 'a redresser of wrongs': someone whose belatedness, whose second-generation inheritance of the throne is rescripted, in the realm of phantasy, as an historical *necessity*.

The mechanism that supports this dream of necessity is, of course, nationalism and its underlying scrim of 'moral values'. It is not surprising that the bill passed a few days after the 9-11 attacks expanding the government's rights to intrude on civil liberties was called 'The Patriot Act'. As Tom Nairn has eloquently argued,

Through nationalism the dead are awakened, this is the point –
seriously awakened for the first time. All cultures have been
obsessed by the dead and placed them in another world.
Nationalism rehouses them in this world. Through its agency
the past ceases being 'immemorial': it gets memorialized into
time present, and so acquires a future. For the first time it is
meaningfully projected on to the screen of futurity.[9]

Let us examine this 'screen of futurity'. On June 6, 2002, George
W. Bush delivered a televised address to Americans, calling for
the establishment of a 'Department of Homeland Security'. The
purpose of this new agency would be to coordinate all offices
essential to national security under one infrastructure and,
according to Bush, 'produce a single daily picture of threats
against our homeland. Analysts will be responsible for imagining
the worst and planning to counter it'. 'History', declared Bush,

> has called our nation into action. History has placed a great
> challenge before us. Will America, with our unique position
> and power, blink in the face of terror, or will we lead to a freer,
> more civilized world? There is only one answer. This great
> country will lead the world to safety, security, peace and
> freedom.[10]

In hypostatizing History as an Uber-agent, a supra-national Big
Other that has issued its 'call' to us, Bush's rhetoric blatantly
resuscitates not the America of the Persian Gulf War but the
America of the Second World War. The dead who are being
awakened are not those victims who died in the terrorist
bombings but the heroes of our nostalgic vision of a simpler,
more innocent time, the heroes who lent us dignity and grandeur
by vanquishing that other 'axis of evil', the fascist Nazis and the
Japanese aggressors.

With these grandiose claims, Bush projects the dead of a glorified
past onto the 'screen of futurity'. No longer about rectifying a
particular situation (Al Quaeda), the 'universal content' is now
about leading the world to a new future *via the past*, fully articulated
in the Bush doctrine of pre-emptive strike, which now includes
not only stateless terrorism but the operations of any sovereign
nation that might someday try to equal America's military
power. This is indeed the preposterous legacy Bush wants to

leave: that the future America will look back at the past Iraq as if it *would have attacked us* had we not invaded first. In projecting the ideological content of a war against terrorism onto a screen of futurity that will 'imagine the worst and plan to counter it', Bush metamorphosed, virtually overnight, from a revenger of actual crimes – September 11 – to a new order of being, a truly Post-modern Hamlet: the Revenger-in-Advance, one who will punish potential enemies *before* they strike.[11]

One of the factors that delays Shakespeare's Hamlet from taking revenge is a desire for conclusive proof of Claudius's guilt. In spite of his 'prophetic soul', Hamlet will have proof more rela-tive than hearsay, even if (and perhaps because) that testimony comes from a ghost who looks just like his father. Unlike Hamlet, who has more evidence of Claudius's guilt than he knows what to do with, for the Revenger-in-Advance it is precisely the *lack* of evidence that confirms his belief in the need for action. On May 29, 2003, George W. Bush announced to the press that 'we found the weapons of mass destruction in Iraq', even though it turned out not to be true. The Downing Street memo (still being largely ignored) implies that the intelligence had been manipu-lated to suit the administration's desire for war. Finally on July 9, 2003, with pressure increasing for disclosure about the lack of evidence, Bush, in a press conference, snapped angrily at reporters: 'Look – I am confident that Saddam Hussein had a weapons of mass destruction program.'

In a *rational* culture, insistence on certainty despite all evidence to the contrary would signal that a leader was either a 'criminal or a mental defective' (Thayer 1983). But I would argue that it was *precisely* this aspect of Bush's character that convinced Americans to re-elect him in 2004. The hypnotic effect of the Postmodern Revenger's *performative* belief lends him the appearance of ideolog-ical sublimity and generates his *charisma*. For the Revenger-in-Advance (with his doctrine of pre-emptive Strike), an enemy is always already guilty on the 'screen of futurity' and therefore the very notion of having to provide proof is offensive. Hard evidence is for rogue and peasant slaves who lack gall to make oppression bitter; for a president who can look into the eyes of foreign leaders and see their souls, it is irrelevant.[12]

The problem with pre-emptive revenge, however, is that it closely resembles totalitarianism – which is never launched openly as the imposition of one subject's imperial will but always as a doctrine of 'higher cause' or 'common good'. As Žižek puts it,

> Totalitarianism...interpellates the subject on behalf of HIS OWN good ('what may appear to you as an external pressure, is really the expression of your objective interests, of what you REALLY WANT without being aware of it').[13]

Totalitarianism traffics in the vague language of moral absolutes dictated from above. 'What seduces us into obeying it is the very feature that may appear to be an obstacle – the absence of a "why"' (Žižek 2000: 120). In this warped but powerful logic, the very insufficiency of the argument (WMD, links to 9-11) *guarantees* the seductive force of the injunction. If one particular set of reasons does not actually pan out, 'decision value' permits an endless series of substitute rationales. What matters is the absolute relationship to moral righteousness being modelled, no matter how fragile that absolute is shown to be. In Bush's Soulocracy – that strange political realm in which good souls can spot evil souls and tell what they are up to – what need one hundred United Nations inspectors? What need fifty? Nay, what need one?[14]

Reason not the need. It is not a big leap from a political Soulocracy to a system in which justice resides not in laws but in intuitions, in the 'prophetic souls' of a few powerful individuals. There is grim irony behind the political exercise of *de facto* monarchy at the start of the new millennium. Thomas Paine, and the framers of the Constitution, argued that there is nothing so dangerous as the fetishizing of an individual leader's character. Paine's words are suitably prophetic here:

> Men who look upon themselves as born to reign, and others to obey, soon grow insolent; selected from the rest of mankind, their minds are early poisoned by importance; and the world they act in differs so materially from the world at large, that they have but little opportunity of knowing its true interests, and when they succeed to the government are frequently the most ignorant and unfit of any throughout the dominions (*Common Sense*, 1776).[15]

When George W. Bush declares that 'History has called our nation into action', what he is really doing is asking us, as

Hamlet asks Horatio at the end of Act 5, to absent ourselves from felicity awhile (however long it takes) and draw our breaths in pain to 'tell his story'; not the story of a son of 'insolence' and privilege, whose mind, in Paine's words, has been 'early poisoned by importance', whose world 'differs so materially from the world at large'; but the story of someone who, in Fortinbras's words, 'prov'd most royal, being put on; and for his passage, / The soldier's music and the rite of war / Speak loudly for him' (5.2.399–401).

Like Hamlet (also never a soldier), George W. Bush asked Americans to do nothing less than disavow our experience of his first four acts – in this case his first four years – and to begin our future story about him in the fifth: to let the 'decision value' of September 11, and the toppling of Saddam, revise everything we have witnessed, and to let his drive for pre-emptive revenge distract us from all the 'collateral damage' that has littered, and continues to litter, the world stage as a result. After all, an American Hamlet, as our 'repository of national life force', must *never have doubts* about what he has done. That a majority of Americans still believe that Saddam Hussein was involved in the September 11 attacks suggests that, for contemporary America, George W. Bush is the right *kind* of revenger, even if he is not revenging the right crime.

In Shakespeare's *Hamlet*, the eventual fulfillment of the ghost's mandate to kill Claudius does not restore integrity to Denmark but rather, the opposite. The wide swath of death inflicted by Hamlet's incompetent revenger-justice has led to the death of his state. From a larger perspective (that of an Elizabethan audience perhaps), this is an unacceptable outcome, one to which centuries of reception to the play seem strangely inured. But if we read the ending of *Hamlet* as I think we should, that is to say, *literally*, we can hear from Shakespeare a warning that resounds to this day: that in order to embrace Horatio's action-Hamlet, we must agree that the death of a nation is an acceptable price to pay for the privilege of worshipping at the shrine of a Crown Prince's so-called Character. When we tell our Revenger's story, will we speak

> Of carnal, bloody, and unnatural acts,
> Of accidental judgements, casual slaughters,

> Of deaths put on by cunning and forced cause;
> And, in this upshot, purposes mistook
> Fall'n on th'inventors' heads?

Perhaps; but it is too soon to know. One thing is certain, however: the doctrine of Divine Right may have changed its costume, but the King has not left the building; nor will he, as long as our Hamlet – like Shakespeare's – believes that there is a divinity that shapes his ends, rough-hew them how he will.

8
Conclusion

The Plot

Hamlet returns from school in Wittenberg to see his father's funeral and his mother's remarriage to his uncle. The Ghost of the dead king appears and tells Hamlet that his uncle Claudius is his murderer. The Ghost commands Hamlet to revenge, and Hamlet, apparently eagerly, agrees. After much delay and 'collateral damage', Hamlet, in his own dying moment, finally kills his uncle. Fortinbras arrives with troops and takes over Denmark. The rest is silence.

With this simple plot Shakespeare bequeaths to us his longest play, a monumental aria on ambivalence, on what one *actively* does by actively *not doing* something else. Hamlet is often regarded as Shakespeare's paragon of psychological complexity. We are privy to Hamlet's extended meditations, his obsessions, his 'innermost thoughts'. But for all their sound and fury, for all the windy suspiration of forced breath it takes to get through his hundreds of lines of soliloquy, Hamlet's interior monologues ultimately tell us very little about who he is or why he behaves as he does.

I would like to close this book with some thoughts about procrastination and preferences. To do so I will require a foil for our prince. The trouble with foils, however, as Richard Levin has recently written, 'is that once one joins the enterprise of foil-hunting, there is no place to stop'.[1] Levin is referring to foils within the play itself; and he argues that Laertes serves as a true dramatic foil for Hamlet. He does go so far as to concede that 'if some critics want to call Fortinbras (or the First Player for that matter) a foil to Hamlet, that seems harmless enough' (ibid.: 226). I fear that Levin will not find my foil so harmless, since not only is this foil not in the play, but he is neither in Shakespeare's corpus nor even in the 'early modern' period. There is an ideal foil for Hamlet; but to hunt him down we have to jump forward 250 years and over the pond.

> *Ah, Bartleby! Ah, Humanity!*
>
> – Herman Melville

In Melville's extraordinary short story *Bartleby the Scrivener: A Story of Wall Street*, published in 1853, the narrator (a self-described 'eminently safe man' and finance lawyer) gives an account of his most disturbing and remarkable employee:

> While, of other law-copyists, I might write the complete life, of Bartleby nothing of that sort can be done. I believe that no materials exist for a full and satisfactory biography of this man. It is an irreparable loss to literature.[2]

An irreparable loss to literature: possibly. But Bartleby is not the first character for whom no materials exist for a full and satisfactory biography.[3] For the sake of closing argument, let us imagine that Melville's Bartleby is the answer, in inverted form (as all replies of the Real are), to the riddle of Shakespeare's Sphinx.

We cannot know whether Melville had Hamlet in mind as he fashioned his strange clerk; but the ultra-'reasonable' narrator does seem to play Horatio to Bartleby's inscrutable subjectivity. Neither the glass of fashion nor the mould of form, Bartleby is 'pallidly neat, pitiably respectable, incurably forlorn!' (ibid.: 105). In an office full of colorful and voluble personalities (nicknamed Turkey, Nippers, and Gingernut), Bartleby stands in stark contrast, performing his duties 'silently, palely, mechanically' (106).

'Meet it is' that Bartleby is a scrivener. Like Hamlet, he is eager – 'famished' the narrator says – to set things down. His lugubriously robotic nature is puzzling but unthreatening until he shows his first unexpected sign of personality. On the third day of his employment, the narrator wishes Bartleby to proof-read a copy of an urgent business document:

Imagine my surprise, nay, my consternation, when without moving from his privacy, Bartleby, in a singularly mild, firm voice, replied, 'I would prefer not to' (107).

Bartleby's employer has given him a mandate, and – like Old Hamlet's Ghost – he expects his subordinate to carry it out. Unlike Prince Hamlet, however, Bartleby refuses not only to comply but, even more perversely, refuses to explain his refusal. It is the lack of explanation that Bartleby's employer finds at once most disturbing and fascinating:

'Why do you refuse?'
'I would prefer not to.'
With any other man I should have flown outright into a dreadful passion, scorned all further words, and thrust him ignominiously from my presence. But there was something about Bartleby that not only strangely disarmed me, but, in a wonderful manner, touched and disconcerted me. I began to reason with him...

'I prefer not to,' he replied in a flute-like tone. It seemed to me that, while I had been addressing him, he carefully revolved every statement that I made; fully comprehended the meaning; could not gainsay the irresistible conclusion; but, at the same time, some PARAMOUNT CONSIDERATION PREVAILED with him to reply as he did (108).

Eventually, as the narrator receives minor variations of the same reply to other requests he makes of his employee – 'I would prefer not to'; 'I prefer not to'; 'at present I would prefer not to' – we begin to feel that Bartleby's 'I' is not such an inconsiderable thing and his 'respectability' not altogether 'pitiable'.

When the narrator, now frankly irritated, asks Bartleby to 'step around to the Post Office... and see if there is anything for me' (111), Bartleby says

'I would prefer not to.'
'You will not?'
'I prefer not' (111).

Bartleby distinguishes between his preference and his 'will'; at no point in the story does he say 'I will not.' His employer, a kindly sort, tempers his anger with forbearance; but eventually his curiosity becomes too intense to resist:

> 'Bartleby,' said I, in a still gentler tone, 'come here; I am not going to ask you to do anything you would prefer not to do – I simply want to speak to you.' Upon this he noiselessly slid into view.
> 'Will you tell me, Bartleby, where you were born?'
> 'I would prefer not to.'
> 'Will you tell me *anything* about yourself?'
> 'I would prefer not to' (116).

The narrator quite reasonably wishes to fire Bartleby; but feels 'something superstitious knocking at [his] heart', something that would 'denounce [him] for a villain if [he] dared to breathe one bitter word against this forlornest of mankind'. Abandoning his efforts to learn anything about Bartleby's history, the narrator 'entreats' him, 'as a friend, to comply as far as may be with the usages of this office' (116):

> 'say now, that in a day or two you will begin to be a little reasonable: – say so Bartleby.'
> 'At present I would prefer not to be a little reasonable,' was his mildly cadaverous reply (117).

Anyone who has read Melville's story cannot help but notice how frequently the narrator uses the word 'will', as if willing were the only form of agency available to a person. Later in the story the narrator hints that Bartleby should leave, tries to pay him to leave, and finally orders him to leave:

> 'Will you, or will you not, quit me?' I now demanded in sudden passion, advancing close to him.
> 'I would prefer *not* to quit you,' he replied, gently emphasizing the *not* (121).

For all of his refusals, Bartleby takes pains to emphasize that it is not that he *will* not comply but that he *prefers* not to. This seems an extremely important detail, one that resonates with implications for *Hamlet*.

Clearly Bartleby exercises his will by privileging his preference. Why then does he refuse to own it *as* 'will'? In his closing soliloquy of 4.4. (before his 'voyage' to England), Hamlet – berating occasions that inform against him and himself for leaving his 'dull revenge' unaccomplished – says:

> ....I do not know
> Why yet I live to say 'This thing's to do,'
> Sith I have cause, and will, and strength, and means
> To do't....
>
> ....Rightly to be great
> Is not to stir without great argument,
> But greatly to find quarrel in a straw
> When honor's at the stake. How stand I, then,
> That have a father killed, a mother stained,
> Excitements of my reason and my blood,
> And let all sleep... (44–47; 54–60).[4]

Hamlet acknowledges – *owns* – that he has cause, and will, and strength, and means, to perform his revenge. Furthermore, he has every reason to be more than a little unreasonable. Possessing, he believes, every element necessary to enable agency, he cannot understand his inability to exercise it. Here of course is where we bump up against the rock of Hamlet's Real, for he seems to be the only one in the play who does not see that his 'will', as Laertes warns Ophelia,

> ....is not his
> own. For he himself is subject to his birth.
> He may not, as unvalued persons do,
> Carve for himself, for on his choice depends
> The safety and health of this whole state,
> And therefore must his choice be circumscribed
> Unto the voice and yielding of that body
> Whereof he is the head (1.2.17–24).

Hamlet may be the 'glass of fashion and the mould of form', as Ophelia says later; but according to Laertes, there is no 'PARA-MOUNT CONSIDERATION' that can outweigh the require-ments of the state on Hamlet's will.

The PARAMOUNT CONSIDERATION that prevails for Bartleby clearly is his 'I', and it remains steadfast. He may not, like Hamlet, have cause or will or strength or means, but he PREFERS and he honors his preference. Bartleby knows so entirely what he prefers that he need not explain himself to others, no matter how 'reasonably' an explanation is requested. This is a supremely powerful act and, however socially damaging the results to him may be, a stark expression of individual sovereignty. Insofar as Bartleby's 'preference' seems to be its own object/cause of desire, it conforms to the logic of the 'Objet A', or Desire in the Lacanian sense. Even if expressed as a negative proposition, we can answer the question 'What does Bartleby want?' He wants to honor his preference not to. Why does he want that? Because it is what he prefers. To give one's own preference pride of first place, regardless of the consequences, is inarguably a form of freedom.

One might object that to admire this is to admire a solipsistic narcissism, an inexplicable selfishness; except that Melville's entire point is that Bartleby *has no self apart from his preference* – it is the only stage upon which a 'self' appears. Bartleby's quiet, mild, unrelenting privileging of the 'I' even in the face of his employer's reasonable, patient, and sympathetic requests is the obverse of Hamlet's radical 'de-selfing'. In 1.5., after the ghost of his father reveals his obscene self-absorption and, with his command to kill Claudius, his complete lack of regard for the fate of his son, Hamlet's response is 'Thy commandment all alone shall live / Within the book and volume of my brain' (103–4).

Hamlet has the cause, will, strength, and means to carry out the ghost's commandment. What he does not have is the preference; or (as I argued in Chapter 5) a sense of *entitlement to* a preference. No matter how vehemently he declares, in 5.1. as he jumps into Ophelia's grave, 'This is I, Hamlet the Dane', we can hear in his syntax the self-gap, the self-withholding, that prevents him from fusing what he wants to what he 'wills'. After all, by now we are in Act 5, and Hamlet *still* has not accomplished his 'dull revenge'. The 'to be or not to be' soliloquy would make more sense as 'to prefer or to prefer not to, that is the question'. But this is the one question Hamlet cannot ask: Do I really want to carry out this *particular* father's commandment, or would I prefer not to? Scandalous to suggest such a thing? Perhaps, but *Hamlet* is a scandalous play. His inability to ask this question – 'what would I prefer?' – takes a different shape, a more 'questionable' shape, as the play's hysterical symptom – pathological delay.

At the end of Act 5, more as a direct response to his mother's death and his own poisoning than to his father's command, Hamlet finally 'prefers' to kill Claudius. At last we may have an answer. To paraphrase Freud: where procrastination is, there shall preference be.

Prince Hamlet, who 'must like a whore unpack [his] heart with words' (2.2.586), cannot stop trying to explain himself whilst Bartleby, several centuries later, refuses to explain anything to anyone. The former presumably has everything – a title, nobility, wealth, intellect, physical grace, privilege; the latter has nothing – no family, no connections, no friends, no charisma, no wealth, no home. In their respective 'social and historical contexts' they could not be more different. But in the heart of their mysteries, they are inverted doubles. Both lack employment (Hamlet displaced from the throne, Bartleby eventually fired and physically removed from the premises). Both are, as Melville's narrator says of Bartleby, 'incurably forlorn'; both traffic, albeit in different forms, in refusal; and for both there is insufficient material for a 'satisfactory biography'.

If we read Hamlet and Bartleby through the 'glass of fashion' – that is, as presentists or historicists, as materialists or poststructuralists – their very different generic, temporal, textual, and geopolitical 'conditions of production' would make it impossible for us to read them as foils. But if we read them through the 'mould of form' (alism), we can easily see that both Hamlet and Bartleby contribute mightily to the same *affective* legacy. As with Hamlet, Bartleby's refusals are a symptom (indeed, for the narrator, Bartleby's 'preferences' can only be a sign of something 'else'). However, as Adam Phillips would put it, Bartleby's symptom is not a 'sign' but 'an experiment in living',[5] whereas Hamlet's symptom is an experiment in not living. The value of reading these singularly striking texts in tandem, across temporal and national boundaries, lies in the questions that *together* they raise about one of the most enduring and important dilemmas in political psychology: What is the most effective form for a refusal to take? What kinds of refusals can help us not (as with Hamlet and arguably with Bartleby) to deny a distasteful past but to create *a usable future*?

I will not segue here into critical moralisms about how we should read texts for their 'pockets of resistance'. I have always thought that nothing can subvert and reaffirm at the same time. If something subverts yet reaffirms power, it is a function of cynical idealism, not resistance. Instead, I wonder about the investments (or lack thereof) we make in our preferences; how hard it is to decide which ones are worth stating and standing by, which ones need to go undercover, and which ones should be set aside altogether for a greater good. I wonder about the usefulness, or destructiveness, of flat-out refusal. I am fascinated with and troubled by how *rarely* we actually come out and say 'I would prefer not to' ... subscribe to certain leaders, politicians, policies, 'mandates', institutions, doctrines, beliefs, wars, methodologies, family dynamics, corporate deceptions, and Supreme Court decisions. It seems to me that in spite of its pathology (or maybe because of it), Bartleby's ability to say 'I would prefer not to' and to act on that preference is an enviable quality. *I would prefer not to* – even if it makes me unpopular, costs me my job, deprives me of my inheritance, robs me of my status, looks unfashionable, confounds my friends, and comforts my enemies, 'I would prefer not to go along with this.'

On the one hand, procrastination, passive resistance, passive aggression, and behind-the-scenes complaining undermine authority; but they undermine self-agency as well and, as Hamlet demonstrates, are not the most effective ways of getting things done. On the other hand, rigid insistence on one's preference in the face of *all good reasons* to the contrary – whether one is Richard II, or Bartleby the Scrivener, or George W. Bush – leads only to destruction, of self and/or others. Maybe everything really does happen 'in the middle'. Does it matter what form refusals take? I think it does. Nonetheless, I like to imagine an alternate universe in which Melville travels back in time, meets Shakespeare, and together they write *Hamlet the Scrivener*.

The Plot:

The Ghost of Hamlet's father tells him that something has been egregiously miscopied, that his story has been improperly transmitted, that it must be corrected, set right, and that his version of the story is the only TRUE VERSION. Young Hamlet (though pallid and incurably forlorn!) has up to this moment been filling his tablet with saws of youth and trivial fond records. 'Wipe it all away,' says the Ghost, 'So that my commandment may live alone in the book and volume' of your brain, unmixed with baser matter.' Hamlet – son, namesake, employee, subject, citizen, legatee, and always copyist, replies: 'The Text is out of joint. Oh, curséd Spite / That ever I was born to set it right...I would prefer not to.'

What does Shakespeare's Hamlet really want? I certainly do not know; but I do know that it is not what he says he wants. Some of our most compelling fictions, Žižek says, 'emerge from the wrong combinations of the elements of our real experience'.[6] What are the 'wrong combinations' of Hamlet's 'real experience'? Maybe a mother and father who loved each other and him, a father for whom the son's existence mattered, a king who had his heir's, and his nation's, best interests at heart, a leader whose deepest concern was with the future of those who would come after him. All of us must deal with the fictions we manufacture about the people who presumably care for us and look after our best interests. As Jeremy Bentham said, it is 'to language alone...that fictitious entities owe their existence – their impossible, indispensable, existence'.[7]

True enough. However, some fictitious entities are more impossible or indispensable than others. And some must simply be flat-out refused, especially the Monarch-Entities whose deformed legacies we will all have to carry into the future unless we decide that we would prefer not to and stand by our preference, come what may. If Horatio ever does manage truly to deliver Hamlet's story, then must he speak of someone who loved not wisely but too well; of someone perplexed in the extreme; and finally of someone who said 'yes' when somewhere, deep down inside, hidden even from himself, he really wanted to say HELL NO. I could probably say more about this...but at present, I would prefer not to.

Ah, Hamlet! Ah, Humanity!

Notes

Chapter 1: Introduction: *Passing Which Torch?*

1. In recent conversation with Barbara Hodgdon about the ongoing
   relevance of the 1990s, she used the phrase a 'moment of origin',
   supporting my sense that, rather than casting perspective backward's
   on the decades that preceded it, the last decade of the millennium
   laid the foundation for the nexus of events which are now being played
   out on the global stage.
2. Sloterdijk's ideas are explored in greater depth in several of the
   essays in this book. Although *A Critique of Cynical Reason* was first
   published in German in 1983 (and translated into English in
   1987), his analysis and coinage of the phenomenon of 'cynical
   idealism' remains one of the most illuminating tools for understanding
   the psychology of contemporary politics in America.
3. Žižek (1989: 29).
4. Nothing has belied the doctrine of 'compassionate conservatism'
   more nakedly than Hurricane Katrina and the flooding of New
   Orleans.
5. When I have given sections of these essays as talks, there have occasionally been one or two people in the audience who object, saying
   'Aren't you generalizing about Americans and American culture? I
   can't locate myself in the America you describe!' I would not expect
   most academics to fit into the mindset I describe; scholars are a tiny
   and unusual percentage of the citizenry. And while I too cannot 'locate
   myself' in the America I describe, things are different in southern
   Indiana than they are, say, in Cambridge, or San Francisco.
   However much they may wish to be exempt from responsibility for
   the failures of government, all Americans are located geopolitically
   in the America that has permitted the current Administration and
   Congress to proceed with their policies.
6. Anyone who watched the now defunct Dennis Miller show on HBO
   will recall Miller's 'Rants', which usually began with 'I don't know
   about you but', followed by a scathing critique of some aspect of

society or politics, and sardonically ended with 'Of course that's just my opinion, and I could be wrong.'

7. Quoted in Žižek (2003: 128).
8. The phrase 'paid-up presentist' is Terence Hawkes'. See Hawkes (2002). In his introduction, Hawkes briefly takes David Kastan to task for positing 'presentists' as 'the Bard's most sinister enemy' (2). In Chapter 2, I will address Kastan's recent critical 'intervention' in more detail. But I think Hawkes does well to assert that 'presentists' are every bit as concerned with history as 'historicists':

> History is far too important to be left to scholars who believe themselves able to make contact with a past unshaped by their own concerns…Paying the present that degree of respect might more profitably be judged, not as a 'mistake', egregious and insouciant, blandly imposing a tritely modern perspective on whatever texts confront it, but rather as the basis of a critical stance whose engagement with the text is of a particular character. A Shakespeare criticism that takes that on board will not yearn to speak with the dead. It will aim, in the end, to talk to the living' (3–4).

9. See Nairn (2000: 199–200).

Chapter 2: The Fetish of 'the Modern'

1. See Bourdieu, *Homo Academicus* (1994).
2. The term 'SmackDown' comes from World Wrestling Entertainment Inc. (WWE), which broadcasts its over-the-top theatrical fights between people in bizarre costumes, with names like Road Warrior Animal, Hardcore Holly, and Rey Mysterio, fighters who often 'stand for' broad ethnic or class divisions. These 'divisions' are caricatured in ways that can only be described as burlesque.
3. See Bruster (2000: 176).
4. For information on the Chinese concept of modernity, I am indebted to conversations with Xiaolin Li, who is Associate Professor of Western and Comparative Literature at Zhejiang University in China. Li was a visiting scholar at Indiana University in the spring of 2004, and her research interests include adaptations of Shakespearean plays into opera.
5. Margreta de Grazia, 'Hamlet Before Its Time' (2001: 360).
6. Richard Halpern (1997: 10). We should differentiate between terms such as 'modernity', and 'modernism', as each indexes a different category of usage. 'Modernism' designates an aesthetic movement – in literature, architecture, the visual arts, dance, and music. Halpern challenges the academic 'assumption that modernism ever ended' (2), and remarks on how 'the prestige of modernism as a literary movement' is responsible for the 'persistence of modernist themes and interpretations' (2). Describing modernism as a form of

'historical allegory' that arises as a 'reaction to the thoroughgoing historicism of nineteenth century thought' (4), Halpern nonetheless sees it as a 'productive resource rather than an embarrassing encumbrance' (10). Adopting a 'modernist' mode that he interprets 'largely in traditional Marxist terms', however (11), Halpern traffics in modernism's formalism while yoking it, by self-definition, to a traditionally Marxist anchor in the conditions of material production. Despite his attempt to end-run around the hegemony of the new historicist method, Halpern continues to accept the modernist allegory as a legitimate way of organizing historical response. The traditional Marxist mode combines historicist referentiality (conditions and modes of production) with the philosophical idealism inherent in historical materialism. This continued insistence on a materialist 'fact-base' in my view makes both modernism and historicism similar hermeneutics.

7. Of course we do not really want other nations to 'catch up' with us; when they do they become 'competition' (China and India, for instance) or a nuclear 'threat'. We will export our version of modernity and democracy as long as we can limit technological development in nations that do not see things our way. Unless of course it is too late, as it is in North Korea, Iran, and Pakistan.

8. Certainly Thomas Paine spelled out the direct relationship between liberty and commerce in *Common Sense*; and the litany of complaints in *The Declaration of Independence* about British commercial, financial, and business constraints on the colonies also makes the connection. But since the Reagan Era, 'liberty', 'freedom', and 'democracy' have become completely synecdochized with trickle-down capitalist economics, and never more so than under the current administration of George W. Bush.

9. See Latour (1993: 25).

10. See Nelson (2001). Interestingly, Nelson does not refer to Latour's work at all, which to my mind makes their respective arguments all the more persuasive. They arrive at virtually the same diagnostic model of western 'modernity' through different hermeneutical channels. What is the secret life of a puppet if not a hybrid between the subject/object poles? Read together, their studies complement each other.

11. Although our 'love affair with realism' has gotten so excessive that it borders on obsession. On Wednesday, July 7, 2005, while the war in Iraq rages on and with the death toll rising steadily with each passing week, television producer Steven Bochco premiered his new television series called 'Over There': a fictionalized, 'personalized' drama about 'characters' – US soldiers in Iraq – and the daily travails of their lives and those of their families. While Bochco has anticipated criticism, he has also 'veined' the drama

'with a message that is cautiously bold: hate war, love the troops' (Alessandra Stanley, *The New York Times*, July 7, 2005: B1). In my view, no matter how critical the show may be of administration policy, turning it into entertainment for Americans to watch after dinner is an implicit acceptance. One wonders whether there will be equal focus in the show on civilian Iraqi family 'characters' and the daily traumas they suffer.

12. See Kastan (1999: 31). Terence Hawkes has also objected to Kastan's caricature of presentism. I see Kastan's confusing formulations less as an attack on presentism *per se* (as Hawkes does) and more as a symptom of the logical contortions some scholars undergo in order to perform their 'interventions' at the expense of others. See Hawkes, *Shakespeare in the Present* (London and New York: Routledge, 2002).

13. Adam Phillips (1997).

14. See Žižek, *On Belief* (2002: 13).

Chapter 3:   Dismember Me: Shakespeare, Paranoia, and the *Noir* World Order

1. Sloterdijk (1987).

2. All references to *Hamlet* are from *The Oxford Shakespeare*, ed. G.R. Hibbard (1987).

3. Cf. Roy Lisker, *Ferment* magazine, March 25, 2003.

4. Žižek (1992: 151).

5. See Lacan, *The Seminar of Jacques Lacan: Book II* (1991: 72).

6. Cf. Slavoj Žižek (1989: 97–101 *passim*).

7. Žižek (1992: 158).

8. Ibid.

9. Ibid.: 159. In the chapter 'Why Are There Only Two Fathers', Žižek mentions *Hamlet* only elliptically on p. 159, before returning to his discussion of Wagner's *Parsifal*. This seems to me to be a symptomatic near-oversight: Žižek notices that the ghost's knowledge 'concerns a dark, licentious side of the father-king who is otherwise presented as an ideal figure'; yet, like Prince Hamlet himself, Žižek proceeds to ignore the implications of this, arguing as he does that paranoiac *noir* emerges as a postwar phenomenon of the twentieth century (cf. pp.149–52 *passim*).

10. I am indebted to Barbara Mowat for questioning my tacit assumption, in an earlier version of this chapter, that there was already on the Renaissance stage a 'tradition' of logic-and-deduction revenging that *Hamlet* breaks with. Rather, as Mowat pointed out to me, there is very little existing textual evidence of a specifically English subgenre of revenge tragedy, apart from Kyd's play, and the purported *Ur-Hamlet*. In our conversations about this matter, we became fascinated that in the light of this slim 'tradition' not only

readers and audiences, but centuries of critics (myself included) had been convinced that *Hamlet* was breaking with a longstanding 'tradition'; and not because of anything much already 'out there' on the English stage but because the play encourages us to identify so fully with Hamlet's *own* sense that he is not living up to established expectation. I hasten here to add that Mowat and I are in complete agreement that there *was* for Shakespeare, as for Kyd, a classical and Latin (Senecan) tradition of revenge tragedy that obviously made its presence felt on the Renaissance stage. But it seems at least as much a function of the play's legerdemain that we feel Prince Hamlet to be breaking with a tradition of English revenge tragedy rather than, as is more accurate, to be inaugurating one. For a thorough and useful discussion/analysis of the western tradition of 'revenging', see John Kerrigan's rich study, *Revenge Tragedy: Aeschylus to Armageddon* (1996), esp. Chapters 5–7. See also Louise Schleiner (1990: 29–48); and Fredson Bowers (1940).

11. See Terence Hawkes' classic essay 'TELMAH' (1985), on the strange recursivity or backward narratologic of *Hamlet*.
12. Žižek (1992: 160).
13. Ibid.: 152.
14. Ibid.: 159–60.
15. Cf. Derrida (1987).
16. Cf. Barbara Klinger (1991: 117–34).
17. Barbara Hodgdon has made a similar observation about the cultural logic of the casting of the film, in which she reads Gibson's body as a female spectator/consumer. For a brilliant analysis on the commercial uses and visual deployments of male bodies, see Hodgdon (1994: 282–8).
18. Gilles Deleuze and Felix Guattari (1983: Chapter 2, *passim*). For several psychoanalytically oriented discussions of *Hamlet* that avoid the rigid limitations outlined by Deleuze and Guattari's critique, see Janet Adelman (1992: 11–37), Marjorie Garber (1987: 125–76), and Ned Lukacher (1986: 178–235). To this list I would also add Jacques Derrida, whose meditation on *Hamlet* and Shakespeare in *Spectres of Marx* (1994: esp. 18–42) is far more Lacanian in 'spirit' than it would appear ('spectres of Lacan', we might even say, given that Lacan's name appears nowhere in the text while Freud's is often invoked).
19. Sloterdijk (1987: 73).
20. I am indebted to Courtney Lehmann for this sharp observation. In a chapter on Hamlet in *Shakespeare Remains*, her wonderful book on 'auteurship' in Shakespeare and film, Lehmann argues 'that Shakespeare's Hamlet has more in common with an aspiring *film noir* director than he does with the reluctant detective of *noir* fiction' (2002: 109).
21. Žižek (1989: 63).

22. Deleuze and Guattari (1983: 115).
23. This term is Joan Copjec's (1994: 27).
24. Herbert Coursen has said something similar about the romantic effect of this moment in Martin's film, in his discussion of different film and televisual treatments of the gravedigger's scene from *Hamlet*. See 'Alas, Poor Yorick!' in *Watching Shakespeare on Television* (1993: 67–8).
25. Hawkes (1985: 316).
26. I am indebted to Carolyn Mitchell for conversations about the racial implications of *LA Story*. I also thank her for bringing de Lauretis's concept of the 'space-off' to my attention in her sharp analysis of the televisual choreography of the Clarence Thomas/Anita Hill hearings. See Mitchell (1993: 190–1) and Teresa de Lauretis (1987: 26).
27. I refer here to the notorious 1990 incident in which Los Angeles police officers savagely beat a black civilian, Rodney King, whom they had chased and stopped for erratic driving. Unbeknownst to the police at the time, a witness videotaped the beating, which when released and broadcast on television news horrified much of the nation (and much of the world) with its intensity and duration. The officers continued brutally to beat King long after he was cowering abjectly on the ground. Two years later, when the officers were finally brought to trial on a charge of excessive force, an all-white jury in Simi Valley, a suburb outside of Los Angeles (in the 'space-off' of Los Angeles proper, we might say) acquitted them. This acquittal triggered the worst racial riots in Los Angeles since those in Watts in the 1960s. In the aftermath of the outcry against the verdict, the two main 'offending' officers were tried on a civil rights charge with regard to the beating and subsequently convicted to brief prison terms.
28. Žižek (1993: 234).

Chapter 4:   We Were Never Early Modern

1. Michael Bristol has written extensively on Shakespeare's marquis value in American mass culture (1996: 1–25).
2. *The Seminar of Jacques Lacan: Book II* (1991: 86).
3. Slavoj Žižek describes the telemetry of ideological fantasy as a proleptic hermeneutic, the 'back to the future' effect of historical and psychoanalytic 'rememoration' (1989: 55–62).
4. See Carolyn Porter's assessment of Foucauldian historicism in literary studies in 'Are We Being Historical Yet?', *South Atlantic Quarterly* 87 (1988): 743–86.
5. In anatomizing the contradictions between the theory and practice of the Modern Constitution, Latour asserts that

No one has ever been modern. Modernity has never begun. There has never been a modern world. The use of the past perfect tense is important here, for it is a matter of a retrospective sentiment, of a rereading of our history. I am not saying that we are entering a new era; on the contrary we no longer have to continue the headlong flight of the post-post-postmodernists; we are no longer obliged to cling to the avant-garde of the avant-garde; we no longer seek to be even cleverer, even more critical, even deeper into the 'era of suspicion'. No, instead we discover that we have never begun to enter the modern era. Hence the hint of the ludicrous that always accompanies postmodern thinkers; they claim to come after a time that has not even started!' (1993: 47).

Chapter 5:   The Hamlet Formerly Known as Prince

Earlier versions and sections of this essay were presented at the Shakespeare Association of America Conference, Cleveland April 1998; and at the Folger Public Lecture in Honor of Shakespeare's Birthday, Washington, D.C., April 1998.

1. There are far more references to *Hamlet* in all forms of contemporary media than I could possibly list here. I will mention two of the more banal appearances, such as the Wendy's commercial in which (the now late) Dave Thomas, wearing a codpiece, does the 'to be or not to be' speech; and the scene at the end of the film *The Big Lebowski*, where John Goodman's character says 'good night, sweet prince, and flights of angels sing thee to thy rest' while sprinkling the ashes of his cremated bowling buddy into the wind. My favourite *Hamlet* citing occurs in a tyre commercial, in which two books are presented to the viewer: a copy of Shakespeare's *Hamlet* and a pamphlet entitled 'Tyre Tips'. The voiceover says: 'One of these offers you timeless wisdom you can use every day of your life. The other is a play.'
2. This quotation is from Bradley Greenburg's (then) unpublished essay 'The Princes Orgulous', to which I was a respondent in the 'Problem Plays' seminar at the 1999 Shakespeare Association of America.
3. All references to the play are from *The Norton Shakespeare*, ed. Stephen Greenblatt (1997).
4. During a Folger Seminar on 'Shakespeare and Postmodernism' that I directed in spring of 1998, I had the occasion to travel by train in and around the Washington, D.C. area. Since to my knowledge, no official survey existed of what people on the street (or on the train or bus) think about *Hamlet*, I polled a captive audience of fellow Amtrak travellers about what – if anything – came to their minds when I mentioned the name Hamlet. I recorded the following: roughly a third said that they had no special associations at all with

the name; others said that Hamlet made them think of romance, England, death, drama, Shakespeare, flunking high school English, poor test scores, Central Park, Kenneth Branagh holding a skull, and men in tights. The one person who said anything at all about plot said 'isn't Hamlet the guy who killed his father?' No one mentioned anything about Hamlet being a prince or the heir to a throne. While this poll is admittedly unscientific, I did speak to people across a range of ages, genders, ethnicities, races, and even nationalities. One person I queried turned out to be a fellow Shakespeare scholar. He declined to comment.

5. A year and a half after I gave a version of this chapter as a talk at the annual meeting of the Shakespeare Association of America in April, 1998, I learned that Margreta de Grazia was working on an essay that made some very similar points about legacy and the lack of a paternal will in *Hamlet*. She was kind enough to send me her essay in page proofs; but by the time I received it my own essay was already in production for inclusion in *Shakespeare and Modernity: Early Modern to Millennium*, ed. Hugh Grady, published by Routledge early in 2000. See de Grazia, 'Weeping for Hecuba' (2000). Although we were unaware of each other's parallel tracks as we were writing, several of our insights are strikingly similar. For example, de Grazia notes that 'only his father's name remains as Hamlet's birthright; the title and entitlement that traditionally attend the patronymic have gone elsewhere' (362). She too discusses at length and in detail the paternity question, the erasure of the female from the transmission of identity, and King Hamlet's failure to leave an official 'will'. Though the aims and approaches of our essays were quite different, we arrived at very complementary conclusions.

6. These definitions are excerpted from longer entries in *The Compact Edition of the Oxford English Dictionary*, 1971: Oxford University Press. See pp. 3269–70 *passim*.

7. Linda Williams analyses 'commodity culture, sexual pleasure, and phallic subjectivity' as they 'interpenetrate in the hard-core porno's money shot' (1989: 106). The 'money shot' is the moment of male ejaculation, captured on film, in which the release of semen is visible to the spectator. According to Williams, the money shot is a fetish in both the Marxian and Freudian senses: 'In combining money and sexual pleasure – those simultaneously valuable and dirty things – the money shot most perfectly embodies the profound alienation of contemporary consumer society' (107). This may be so, but I would argue that the conflation of semen and money is certainly not the product of contemporary alienation – it has a long juridical history, encoded in patriarchal property and sexual relations.

8. This phrase was immortalized by the 'professional football player', played by Cuba Gooding Jr, in the 1997 film *Jerry McGuire*.

9. Eric Mallin (1996) notes that 'The Ghost of King Hamlet tells the heir apparent many things in their first interview, but the political status of the youth goes conspicuously unmentioned; both royal Hamlets seem concerned about things other than the legalities of the succession. The Ghost never protests young Hamlet's loss of position, only his own. Nor does Hamlet himself, for most of the play, lament his preemption from rule' (1996: 111). Mallin speculates that Hamlet's 'disinterest' in his political inheritance is disingenuous: since avenging someone else's murder presumably requires a lack of self-interest, Hamlet could not also actively pursue the crown, since that would decidedly be an example of the reverse. Throughout this chapter, Mallin elegantly weaves the thematics of Elizabethan succession anxieties with the problems of theatrical genre and the demands of scripting a tragedy versus a 'history'.

10. Marjorie Garber discusses the way in which the failure of the 'paternal metaphor' is 'not unrelated to what might be called paternal undecidability, or the undecidability of paternity – the fact, so often commented on in Shakespeare's plays, that the father is always a suppositional father (1987: 132–3). In Garber's view, 'confronted with an overplus, a superfluity of fathers (psychoanalytic readers all comment on the splitting of the father into Claudius, Polonius, even old Fortinbras and old Norway), Hamlet finds both too many fathers and too few' (133).

11. Shakespeare knows how to imply resemblance between fathers and sons. Recall *1 Henry IV*, in which Falstaff, 'play-acting' King Henry IV, addresses his mad wag 'son' Hal:

> That thou art my son I have partly thy mother's word, partly my own opinion, but chiefly a villainous trick of thine eye, and a foolish hanging of thy nether lip, that doth warrant me (2.5.367–70).

12. No body of work represents this principle more completely than the *Henriad*, in which a son who plans to inherit the throne must do whatever it takes *not* to resemble a usurper father. In *Henry V*, 'King Harry' commits affective parricide, turning his father into a kind of ghost. And within the historical logic of the second tetralogy, this 'exchange' works quite nicely. But *Hamlet* offers no such strategy; faced with a 'real' ghost who insists that Hamlet 'remember' him, Hamlet can only lapse into paralysis.

Chapter 6: It's the Monarchy, Stupid

1. Anthony Howard, *The New York Times*, June 5, 2002: A10.
2. Bogdanor, *The Guardian* #47830, July 2000.
3. All references to *Richard II*, *1* and *2 Henry IV*, and *Henry V* are from *The Norton Shakespeare*, ed. Stephen Greenblatt (1997).

4. Cf. Bruno Latour (1993). I discuss Latour's argument about 'The Modern Constitution' at length in Chapter 2, so I will make shortened reference to it here and will concentrate mostly on his notion of 'the Crossed-Out God'.
5. Nairn (1997: 103).
6. Thayer (1983: 22–50, *passim*). For Thayer, Richard's behaviour is less a deliberate flouting of the nobles than a playing by the 'rules of his game', rules that Francis Bacon would put in the simplest of terms in 1600: 'that by the common law of England, a Prince can do no wrong' (22). In this view, 'Richard is not really violating a rule of his game because for him divine kingship has nothing to do with lineal succession (except perhaps his own succession as son of the Black Prince); it is not even a purely secular political convenience' (29). However, as Thayer admits,

> In a political world that has no provision for periodic democratic elections, lineal succession is sensible enough, provided there is some way to prevent a criminal or a mental defective from inheriting the throne. Divine kingship is another matter, and when one tries to attach it inseparably to the principle of lineal succession, one has a potentially poisonous combination, a sort of political theology that sanctions any kind of regal malfeasance (ibid.: 30).

Potentially poisonous certainly, but lineal succession as a 'secular political convenience' has always been insufficient without a reinforcing theology of some kind, whether of divine anointment, or any of its later historical forms, such as 'Manifest Destiny' or other justifying doctrines of racial, gender, or class superiority. Inheritance alone has never been enough to place the monarchy 'beyond argument'.
7. *Op.cit.* (1983: 28–31). Thayer argues that while the point of York's speech is clear, 'Richard never sees the point' (30). Obviously I disagree.
8. See Frye (1988: 113).
9. Cf. MacDonald (1999: 60).
10. Margreta de Grazia (1999: 38–52) argues that 'Elizabethans did not deem language perfect' but rather, 'adequate' (39). De Grazia argues against reading the language of history in the play in 'Post Romantic terms'; but she concedes that 'the seventeenth century abounds in evidence of linguistic pessimism', and notes that even Hobbes (who knew better than anyone the constitutive power of discourse) 'suspects words of subverting political order' (43). If we hold that the seventeenth century does not literally 'begin' until after 1600, I suppose I would agree with de Grazia. However, I do think that Shakespeare was 'ahead of his time' if not in his use of language, then, in his intuitions about the potential political psychology that will lead eventually to democracy.

11. Richard's overly rapid surrender in 3.3. and his alacrity to participate in his un-crowning in 4.1 have often served as platforms for
psychological or psychoanalytic readings of his character. The best
of these in my view is Harry Berger's (1989). Berger argues that
Richard uses Bolingbroke as a 'scapegoat who carries off Richard's
guilt and self-affright' (1989: 73). For Berger, Richard is afflicted
with 'inward wars': a nagging cynical despair that turns him into a
genius of Renaissance self-punishing (1989: 47–55). However we
construe Richard's ultimate goal in this scene, Berger is right that
'whatever we impute to Richard at either the intentional or the
motivational level, his actions as well as his language *dare* Bolingbroke
to assume the usurper's role' (55). Others, from Walter Pater on,
have seen it as Richard's effort to create a wholly new ritual – one
as yet 'unavailable to his culture': the self-decoronation. See Graham
Holderness (2000: 202). See as well Barbara Hodgdon's excellent
study *The End Crowns All: Closure and Contradiction in Shakespeare's
History* (1991). For an interesting and sophisticated discussion of the
difficulty of reading Bolingbroke's 'psychology' and the opacity of
his 'motives', see Nicholas Grene (2002: Chapter 3 *passim*).
12. Slavoj Žižek (1991: 68). For Žižek's discussion of Kantian ethics,
see Žižek (1993: Chapter 3 *passim*).
13. It is frightening how closely Bolingbroke and crew, in this logic,
correspond functionally with Osama bin Laden and Al Quaeda,
insofar as a president whose 'election' required 'Supreme' intervention was only felt to be truly 'legitimate' after external negation
was mobilized against him and the nation by terrorists.
14. If it is true, as Lacan claims in *The Seminar, Book II*, that speech is
'mother to the misrecognised part of the subject', then both
Richard and Bolingbroke speak in ways that run counter to their
apparent intentions. Each occupies a relation to the 'big Other' of
Divine Right; for each, the Doctrine occupies a position analogous
to that of an imaginary analyst insofar as it mobilizes transference
in both Richard and Bolingbroke. Their responses to the Doctrine
are what 'interprets the subject to himself'. Richard's address to the
Analyst/Big Other is 'I am King, I can exercise absolute power of
Divine Right in real political practice.' The Big Other returns his
message in inverted form: you will not truly *be* King until you are
externally deprived of real political power. Bolingbroke's address
to the Analyst/Big Other is 'I do not believe in the symbolic transcendence of Divine Right.' To him, the Big Other replies: then
Divine Right will never believe in you.
15. See Grady's excellent study, *Shakespeare, Machiavelli, and Montaigne:
Power and Subjectivity from Richard II to Hamlet* (2002: 65).
16. Georges Bataille (1985), in his analysis of the psychological effec-
tiveness of fascism, differentiates between two modes of cultural

production that must be kept in careful balance in order for a political system to remain stable. The 'homogeneous' world works conservatively to affiliate social and economic elements within a predictable, and conventionally recognizable, mode of social production. The 'heterogeneous' world 'includes every-thing resulting from unproductive expenditure (sacred things themselves form a part of this whole). This consists of everything rejected by homogeneous society as waste or as superior tran-scendent value' (1985: 142).

17. See Andrew Murphy (2002: 73).

18. In his introduction to *Political Psychology* (1993), Jon Elster makes an important distinction between 'typologies of regimes' and 'catalogues of mechanisms' (2). What Bataille would refer to as the heteroge-neous, or sacralizing irrational element of political psychology, or what Žižek would call the 'anti-descriptivist' element or 'primal baptism' (1989), Elster (more reductively) calls 'nomological thinking' (2). The counterpoint to such thinking is not necessarily complete demystification but something in between 'these two extremes . . . a mechanism is a specific causal pattern that can be recognized after the event but rarely foreseen' (3).

19. See Donald Hedrick (*PMLA*, May 2003). While Hedrick is right that *Henry V* 'performs history as variously advantageable affective labor' (477), I believe it is less at the service of the nascent capitalist agenda Hedrick sees and more about the daunting question of how to reassemble sublimity through the lens of 'cynical idealism'. For another view of the play, see as well Courtney Lehmann's rich and complex discussion of Branagh's film version of *Henry V* and Branagh's repetition-compulsion to rescript his own 'frontier iden-tity' (his relationship to his Irishness) 'through Henry's Welsh facade' (Lehmann 2002: 209).

20. See Hawkes (2002: 37).

21. Kevin Phillips (2002).

22. Cf. K. Phillips, *The Nation*, July 8, 2002: 11.

23. The compromise worked out under Blair was to eliminate hereditary voting rights and replace it with 'Life Peerage' which would not survive its recipient. As Nairn puts it,

> The Blairites decided to abolish hereditary-right voting, while retaining institution. Instead of moving over to an elected Senate in the classical pattern, the Life-Peer principle was to be evolved farther. These Lords-for-a-day would become, in effect, like a working extension of the Monarchy – a ceremonial political guard-room, permitted to tut-tut about legislation and counsel to their hearts' content but without even vestigial powers of interference (2000: 69).

Chapter 7:   Operation Enduring Hamlet

1. Slavoj Žižek (1989).
2. Sloterdijk (1987: 51).
3. For a detailed discussion of the difference between chronological and affective time, cf. Chapter 3 of this book.
4. Ernesto Laclau, quoted in Žižek (2000: 178).
5. Elster (1993: 9).
6. Cf. Jacques Lacan (1993: chapter 21 *passim*).
7. *New York Times* January 26, 2003: Op-Ed.
8. No one, that is, except Condoleeza Rice, George Tenet, and others at the FBI who had received early intelligence reports in July and August 2001 that told of a plot to hijack airliners and fly them into US targets.
9. Tom Nairn (1997: 4).
10. George W. Bush, quoted in *The New York Times*, June 7, 2002: A18.
11. The political psychology I am describing seems impervious to facts. It does not seem to matter that no WMDs were found, just as Joseph Wilson's 2003 debunking of the rumour that Iraq was seeking to purchase uranium from Niger also did not make a difference. The Downing Street memo did not make a dent in this logic either. And the current 'scandal' about the 'outing' of Valerie Plame, Wilson's wife, as a CIA agent revolves not around the revelation that the administration's reasons for invading Iraq were trumped up but around the fact that the White House denied any role in the 'leak' to the press. The 'scandal' is over Karl Rove's role in the leak, not the President's role in lying to the American people about reasons for invading Iraq. Another example of pseudoequivalence.
12. This aspect of presidential judgement is consistent on all fronts. Informing the press about his nomination of John G. Roberts for the US Supreme Court in late July 2005, Bush said 'I've talked to the man. He has a good heart.'
13. Slavoj Žižek (2001: 119).
14. Meanwhile, on October 29, 2004, Osama bin Laden, alive and still on the loose, sends a communique a few days before the 2004 presidential election.
15. Thomas Paine, *Common Sense* (Penguin, 1986: 79).

Chapter 8:   Conclusion

1. See Richard Levin (2002: 226).
2. *American Short Stories*, ed. Eugene Current-García and Walton R. Patrick (1982).
3. Although not for lack of effort, in Hamlet's case. See John Updike's *Gertrude and Claudius* (New York: Knopf, 2000). Updike's novel, the

bookjacket tells us, gives us the 'backstory' to the Hamlet family, and Updike

> brings to life Gertrude's girlhood as the daughter of King Rorik, her arranged marriage to the man who becomes King Hamlet, and her middle-aged affair with her husband's younger brother. Gaps and inconsistencies within the immortal play are to an extent filled and explained in this prequel [dust jacket copy].

4. All references to Hamlet are taken from William Shakespeare, *Hamlet*, ed. Constance Jordan (Pearson Longman 2004).
5. See Adam Phillips' brilliant essay on Melville's *Bartleby* in the context both of psychoanalytic thought and his own clinical experiences dealing with anorexic patients and their personal allegories of refusal. The essay is entitled 'On Eating, and Preferring Not To', in *Promises, Promises* (Phillips 2001).
6. See Žižek (1993: 86).
7. Bentham is quoted in Žižek (1993: 87).

Bibliography

Adelman, Janet. (1992) *Suffocating Mothers*, London and New York: Routledge.

Alter, Jonathan. (1999) 'Huddling against History,' *Newsweek*, 26 July: 50–3.

American Short Stories (1982) ed. Eugene Current-García and Walton R. Patrick, Scott, Foresman and Co.

Anderson, Benedict. (1991) *Imagined Communities*, London: Verso.

Barker, Francis. (1984) *The Tremulous Private Body: Essays in Subjection*, London: Methuen.

Bataille, Georges. (1985) *Visions of Excess: Selected Writings, 1927–1939*, ed. Allan Stoekl, trans. Allan Stoekl, Carl R. Lovitt and Donald M. Leslie, Jr, Minneapolis: University of Minnesota Press.

Baudrillard, Jean. (1993) *The Transparency of Evil: Essays on Extreme Phenomena*, trans. James Benedict, London and New York: Verso.

Berger, Harry. (1989) *Imaginary Audition: Shakespeare on Stage and Page*, Berkeley and Los Angeles: University of California Press.

Bewes, Timothy. (1997) *Cynicism and Postmodernity*, London and New York: Verso.

Bogdanor, Vernon. (2000) quoted in *The Guardian* #47830, July 2, 2000.

Bourdieu, Pierre. (1994) *Homo Academicus*, trans. Peter Collier, Stanford: Stanford University Press.

Bouwsma, William. (1990) *A Usable Past: Essays in European Cultural History*, Berkeley and Los Angeles: University of California Press.

Bowers, Fredson. (1940) *Elizabethan Revenge Tragedy 1587–1642*, Princeton, New Jersey: Princeton University Press.

Bristol, Michael. (1996) *Big Time Shakespeare*, New York and London, Routledge.

Bruster, Douglas. (2000) 'Shakespeare and the End of History: Period as Brand Name', in *Shakespeare and Modernity: Early Modern to Millennium*, ed. Hugh Grady, London and New York: Routledge.

Butler, Judith. (1993) *Bodies That Matter*, New York and London: Routledge.

Copjec, Joan. (1997) *Read My Desire: Lacan Against the Historicists*, Cambridge, MA: MIT Press.

Coursen, Herbert. (1993) *Watching Shakespeare on Television*, Fairleigh Dickinson.

de Grazia, Margreta. (1999) 'Shakespeare's View of Language', in *Shakespeare and History*, eds Stephen Orgel and Sean Keilen, New York and London: Garland Press.

—— (2000) 'Weeping for Hecuba', in *Historicism, Psychoanalysis and Early Modern Culture*, eds Carla Mazzio and Douglas Trevor, New York and London: Routledge.

—— (2001) 'Hamlet Before Its Time', in *Modern Language Quarterly* 62:4.

de Lauretis, Teresa. (1987) *Technologies of Gender: Essays on Theory, Film and Fiction*, Bloomington and Indianapolis: Indiana University Press.

Deleuze, Gilles. (1995) *Difference and Repetition*, trans. Paul Patton, New York: Columbia University Press.

Deleuze, Gilles and Guattari, Felix. (1983) *Anti-Oedipus: Capitalism and Schizophrenia*, Minneapolis: University of Minnesota Press.

Derrida, Jacques. (1987) *The Postcard: From Socrates to Freud and Beyond*, trans. Alan Bass, Chicago: University of Chicago Press.

—— (1994) *Specters of Marx: The State of the Debt, the Work of Mourning, and the New International*, trans. Peggy Kamuf, London and New York: Routledge.

Elster, Jon. (1993) *Political Psychology*, Cambridge, England: Cambridge University Press.

Fineman, Joel. (1989) 'The History of the Anecdote: Fiction and Fiction,' *The New Historicism*, ed. H. Aram Veeser, London and New York: Routledge.

Frank, Thomas. (2004) *What's the Matter With Kansas*, Metropolitan Press.

Frye, Northrop. (1988) 'Richard II and Bolingbroke', in *William Shakespeare's Richard II*, ed. Harold Bloom, New Haven: Yale University Press.

Garber, Marjorie. (1987) *Shakespeare's Ghost Writers: Literature as Uncanny Causality*, New York and London: Methuen.

Grady, Hugh. (2000) *Shakespeare and Modernity: Early Modern to Millennium*, New York and London: Routledge.

—— (2002) *Shakespeare, Machiavelli, and Montaigne: Power and Subjectivity from Richard II to Hamlet*, Oxford: Oxford University Press.

Grene, Nicholas. (2002) *Shakespeare's Serial History Plays*, Cambridge, England: Cambridge University Press.

Halpern, Richard. (1997) *Shakespeare Among the Moderns*, Ithaca: Cornell University Press.

Hawkes, Terence. (1985) '*TELMAH*', in *Shakespeare and the Question of Theory*, eds Patricia Parker and Geoffrey Hartman, New York and London: Routledge.

—— (2002) *Shakespeare in the Present*, London and New York: Routledge.

Hedrick, Donald. (2003) 'Advantage, Affect, History, Henry V', in *PMLA* 118:3.

Hibbard, G.R. (1987) *The Oxford Shakespeare*, Oxford: Oxford University Press.

Hodgdon, Barbara. (1991) *The End Crowns All: Closure and Contradiction in Shakespeare's History*, Princeton: Princeton University Press.

—— (1994) 'The Critic, the Poor Player, Prince Hamlet, and the Lady in the Dark', in *Shakespeare Reread: The Texts in New Contexts*, ed. Russ McDonald, Ithaca: Cornell University Press.

—— (1998) *The Shakespeare Trade: Performances and Appropriations*, Philadelphia: University of Pennsylvania Press.

Holderness, Graham. (2000) *Shakespeare: The Histories*, New York: St. Martin's Press.

Jameson, Fredric. (1991) *Postmodernism or, The Cultural Logic of Late Capitalism*, Durham: Duke University Press.

Jardine, Lisa. (1996) *Reading Shakespeare Historically*, New York and London: Routledge.

Kastan, David. (1999) *Shakespeare After Theory*, London and New York: Routledge.

Kerrigan, John. (1996) *Revenge Tragedy: Aeschylus to Armageddon*, Oxford and New York: Oxford University Press.

Kipnis, Laura. (1998) 'Adultery,' *Critical Inquiry* 21, 2: 289–327.

Klinger, Barbara. (1991) 'Digressions at the Cinema: Commodification and Reception in Mass Culture', in *Modernity and Mass Culture*, eds James Naremore and Patrick Brantlinger, Bloomington: Indiana University Press.

Lacan, Jacques. (1991) *The Seminar of Jacques Lacan, Book I: Freud's Papers on Technique 1953–1954*, ed. Jacques-Alain Miller, trans. John Forrester, New York and London: Norton.

—— (1993) *The Seminar of Jacques Lacan: Book II: The Ego in Freud's Theory and in the Technique of Psychoanalysis 1954–1955*, ed. Jacques-Alain Miller, trans. Sylvana Tomaselli, New York and London: Norton.

Laclau, Ernesto and Mouffe, Chantal. (1989) *Hegemony and Socialist Strategy: Towards a Radical Democratic Politics*, London and New York: Verso.

Latour, Bruno. (1993) *We Have Never Been Modern*, Cambridge, MA: Harvard University Press.

Lehmann, Courtney. (2002) *Shakespeare Remains: Theater to Film, Early Modern to Postmodern*, Ithaca: Cornell University Press.

Levin, Richard. (2002) 'Hamlet, Laertes, and the Dramatic Function of Foils', in *'Hamlet': New Critical Essays*, ed. Arthur Kinney, New York and London: Routledge.

Lukacher, Ned. (1986) *Primal Scenes: Literature, Philosophy, Psychoanalysis*, Ithaca: Cornell University Press.

MacDonald, Ronald R. (1999) 'Uneasy Lies: Language and History in Shakespeare's Lancastrian Tetralogy, in *Shakespeare and History*, ed. Stephen Orgel and Sean Keilen, New York and London: Garland Press, 1999.

Mallin, Eric. (1996) *Inscribing the Time: Shakespeare and the End of Elizabethan England*, Berkeley, CA: University of California Press.

Mitchell, Carolyn. (1993) 'Choicelessness as Choice: The Conflation of Racism and Sexism,' in *Discovering Difference: Contemporary Essays in American Culture*, ed. Christoph K. Lohmann, Bloomington and Indianapolis: Indiana University Press.

Murphy, Andrew. (2002) 'Revising Criticism: Ireland and the British Model', in *British Identities and English Renaissance Literature*, ed. David J. Baker and Willy Maley, Cambridge, England: Cambridge University Press.

Nairn, Tom. (1997) *Faces of Nationalism: Janus Revisited*, London: Verso.

—— (2000) *After Britain: New Labour and the Return of Scotland*, London: Granta Books.

Nelson, Victoria. (2001) *The Secret Life of Puppets*, Cambridge, Mass: Harvard University Press.

Phillips, Adam. (1997) *Terrors and Experts*, Cambridge, MA: Harvard University Press.

—— (2001) *Promises, Promises: Essays on Psychoanalysis and Literature*, Basic Books.

Phillips, Kevin. (2002) *Wealth and Democracy: A Political History of the American Rich*, New York: Broadway Books.

Porter, Carolyn. (1988) 'Are We Being Historical Yet?, *South Atlantic Quarterly* 87.

Schleiner, Louise. (1990) 'Latinized Greek Drama in Shakespeare's Writing of *Hamlet*,' *Shakespeare Quarterly* 41.

Serres, Michel, with Latour, Bruno. (1998) *Conversations on Science, Culture, and Time*, trans. Roxanne Lapidus, Ann Arbor: University of Michigan Press.

Shakespeare, William. (1987) *Hamlet*, ed. G. R. Hibbard, Oxford and New York: Oxford University Press.

——(2004) *Hamlet*, ed. Constance Jordan, Pearson Longman.

——(1997) *Norton Shakespeare, Complete Works*, ed. Stephen Greenblatt, London and New York: Norton.

Sloterdijk, Peter. (1987) *Critique of Cynical Reason*, trans. Michael Eldred, Minneapolis: University of Minnesota Press.

Sohmer, S. (1996) 'Certain speculations on *Hamlet*, the Calendar, and Martin Luther,' *Early Modern Literary Studies* 2, 1:5, 1–51.

Strohm, Paul. (1996) 'The Trouble with Richard: The Reburial of Richard II and Lancastrian Symbolic Strategy,' *Speculum* 71.

Thayer, C.G. (1983) *Shakespearean Politics: Government and Misgovernment in the Great Histories*, Athens, Ohio and London: Ohio University Press.

Updike, John. (2000) *Gertrude and Claudius*, New York: Knopf.

Williams, Linda. (1989) *Hard Core: Power, Pleasure, and the 'Frenzy of the Visible'*, Berkeley, University of California Press.

Wilson, Edgar. (1989) *The Myth of British Monarchy*, London: Journeyman Press.

Wilson, Richard. (1993) *Will Power*, Detroit: Wayne State Press.

Žižek, Slavoj. (1989) *The Sublime Object of Ideology*, London: Verso.

—— (1991) *For They Know Not What They Do: Enjoyment as a Political Factor*, London: Verso.

—— (1992) *Enjoy Your Symptom! Jacques Lacan in Hollywood and Out*, New York and London, Routledge.

—— (1993) *Tarrying With the Negative: Kant, Hegel, and the Critique of Ideology*, Durham: Duke University Press.

—— (1996) *The Indivisible Remainder*, London: Verso.

—— (1999) *The Ticklish Subject*, London: Verso.

—— (2000) *The Fragile Absolute*, London: Verso.

—— (2001) *On Belief*, London and New York: Routledge.

—— (2003) *The Puppet and the Dwarf*, Cambridge, MA: MIT Press.

Index

eBooks – at www.eBookstore.tandf.co.uk

A library at your fingertips!

eBooks are electronic versions of printed books. You can store them on your PC/laptop or browse them online.

They have advantages for anyone needing rapid access to a wide variety of published, copyright information.

eBooks can help your research by enabling you to bookmark chapters, annotate text and use instant searches to find specific words or phrases. Several eBook files would fit on even a small laptop or PDA.

NEW: Save money by eSubscribing: cheap, online access to any eBook for as long as you need it.

Annual subscription packages

We now offer special low-cost bulk subscriptions to packages of eBooks in certain subject areas. These are available to libraries or to individuals.

For more information please contact webmaster.ebooks@tandf.co.uk

We're continually developing the eBook concept, so keep up to date by visiting the website.

www.eBookstore.tandf.co.uk

Related titles from Routledge

World-Wide Shakespeares
Edited by Sonia Massai

World-Wide Shakespeares brings together an international team of leading scholars in order to explore the appropriation of Shakespeare's plays in film and performance around the world. In particular, the book explores the ways in which adapters and directors have put Shakespeare into dialogue with local traditions and contexts.

The contributors look in turn at 'local' Shakespeares for local, national and international audiences, covering a range of English and foreign appropriations that challenge geographical and cultural oppositions between 'centre' and 'periphery', 'big-time' and 'small-time' Shakespeares. Their specialist knowledge of local cultures and traditions make the range of appropriations newly accessible – and newly fascinating – for world-wide readers. Drawing upon debates around the global/local dimensions of cultural production and on Pierre Bourdieu's notion of the 'cultural field', the contributors together demonstrate a significant new approach to intercultural appropriations of Shakespeare.

ISBN10: 0–415–32455–6 (hbk)
ISBN10: 0–415–32456–4 (pbk)

ISBN13: 978–0–415–32455–7 (hbk)
ISBN13: 978–0–415–32456–4 (pbk)

Available at all good bookshops
For ordering and further information please visit:
www.routledge.com

Related titles from Routledge

Local Shakespeares: Proximations and Power
Martin Orkin

'*Local Shakespeares* shows just how timid and predictable most comparative criticism is. Timid and predictable, *Local Shakespeares* is not.'

Bruce Smith, University of Southern California, USA

This remarkable volume challenges scholars and students to look beyond a dominant European and North American 'metropolitan bank' of Shakespeare knowledge. As well as revealing the potential for a new understanding of Shakespeare's plays, Martin Orkin explores a fresh approach to issues of power, where 'proximations' emerge from a process of dialogue and challenge traditional notions of authority.

Since their first performances, Shakespeare's plays and their audiences or readers have journeyed to one another across time and space, to and from countless and always different historical, geographical and ideological locations. Engagement with a Shakespeare text always entails in part, then, cultural encounter or clash, and readings are shaped by a reader's particular location and knowledge. Part I of this book challenges us to recognise the way in which 'local' or 'non-metropolitan' knowledge and experiences might extend understanding of Shakespeare's texts and their locations. Part II demonstrates the use of local as well as metropolitan knowledge in exploring the presentation of masculinity in Shakespeare's late plays. These plays themselves dramatise encounters with different cultures and, crucially, challenges to established authority.

Challenging the authority of metropolitan scholarship, twenty-first-century global capitalism and the masculinist imperatives that drive it, Orkin's daring, powerful work will have reverberations throughout but also well beyond the field of Shakespeare studies.

ISBN10: 0–415–34878–1 (hbk)
ISBN10: 0–415–34879–X (pbk)

ISBN13: 978–0–415–34878–2 (hbk)
ISBN13: 978–0–415–34879–9 (pbk)

Available at all good bookshops
For ordering and further information please visit:
www.routledge.com

Related titles from Routledge

Shakespeare, Authority, Sexuality
Unfinished Business in Cultural Materialism
Alan Sinfield

'Alan Sinfield has been one of the most thoughtful and provocative writers on early modern culture for the last two decades and his critical power is evident throughout this book.'

Kate McLuskie, Director of the Shakespeare Institute,
Stratford-upon-Avon, UK

Shakespeare, Authority, Sexuality is a powerful reassessment of cultural materialism as a way of understanding the intersections of textuality, history, culture and politics by one of the founding figures of this critical movement. Alan Sinfield examines cultural materialism both as a body of ongoing argument, and as it informs particular works by Shakespeare and his contemporaries, especially in relation to sexuality in early-modern England and queer theory.

The book has several interlocking preoccupations:

- Theories of textuality and reading
- Authority in Shakespearean Plays and in the organisation of literary culture today
- The sex/gender system in that period and the application of queer theory in history

These preoccupations are explored in and around a range of works by Shakespeare and his contemporaries. Throughout the book Sinfield re-presents cultural materialism, framing it not as a set of propositions, as has often been done, but as a cluster of unresolved problems. His brilliant, lucid and committed readings demonstrate that the 'unfinished business' of cultural materialism – and Sinfield's work in particular – will long continue to produce new questions and challenges for the field of Renaissance Studies.

ISBN10: 0–415–40235–2 (hbk)
ISBN10: 0–415–40236–0 (pbk)

ISBN13: 978–0–415–40235–4 (hbk)
ISBN13: 978–0–415–40236–1 (pbk)

Available at all good bookshops
For further information on our literature series, please visit
www.routledge.com/literature/series.asp
For ordering and further information please visit:
www.routledge.com